The Transferable Skills of Theatre

50 Monologues
On the use of Theatre Skills
in 50 Common
Occupations and Professions

5-8 Minutes Each
Appropriate for College, High School, and
Advanced Middle School

Monologues

Monologue #1 Landscape-Gardener
Monologue #2 Accountant
Monologue #3 Hairdresser/Beautician/Cosmetologist
Monologue #4 Physician
Monologue #5 Computer Programmer
Monologue #6 Guitar Player/Singer
Monologue #7 Tugboat Captain
Monologue #8 Hotel Manager
Monologue #9 Automobile Salesperson
Monologue #10 Event Promoter
Monologue #11 Basketball Coach
Monologue #12 Graphics Artist
Monologue #13 Sales Account Manager
Monologue #14 Technical Writer
Monologue #15 Postal Worker
Monologue #16 Flight Attendant
Monologue #17 Police Officer
Monologue #18 Fruit and Vegetable Department Manager
Monologue #19 Veterinary Assistant
Monologue #20 Carpenter
Monologue #21 Bus Driver
Monologue #22 Health Inspector
Monologue #23 Personal Assistant
Monologue #24 Human Resources Manager
Monologue #25 Lawyer
Monologue #26 Marine Biologist
Monologue #27 Detective
Monologue #28 Exercise Trainer
Monologue #29 Financial Consultant
Monologue #30 Counselor/Psychologist

Monologue #1 Landscape-Gardener

Hi. Are you the student here for the interview I agreed to? Good. It's a pleasure to meet you. I thought this job site, which is this house under construction, would be the perfect place since I can show you instead of just telling you about what I do. Now, just to be clear, you want to know about the skills I learned in theatre studies and how they have transferred to my profession?

Okay, I will start with my background, and then we will walk around the yard. Most of the schools I attended had a theatre program. I took a few parts here and there. I have a decent singing voice, but I mainly got involved with the technical side of theatre. I've always preferred to work with my hands, you see. I helped build sets. I helped with lighting. Helped move props. After high school, I studied landscaping at a technical school, and I took theatre electives and participated in productions.

Now then, if you will put on this hard hat and step this way, we will start with the garden at the front of the house. I see the garden as a stage. Each plant is an actor. Some plants have lead roles, others have supporting roles. The plants tell the story of the seasons. It's really quite a show. I learned a lot about color and lighting in my theatre studies, which colors complement, which contrast, that sort of thing, and I arrange the flowers accordingly. You see how the purple lavender compliments the yellow daisies?

Now follow me around to the right side of the house. Theatre taught me about framing things, how objects look from different perspectives, and that is why I planted elephant ears along the bottom of the fence and have introduced vines that will climb all the way to the top. That will make the wall seem a natural part of the landscape. The elephant ears will give the visible parts a better proportion.

Here in the backyard I dug into the natural slope to make an area to entertain guests. You will notice that it is a very small amphitheatre. Watching the cooking on the grill will be the main show, but an outdoor TV screen can be set up for sports or whatever. There's something about an amphitheatre that brings people together.

On the far back end of the lawn, I dug a pond and set up a bird bath and a bird feeder. That area is in a corner that is most visible from the kitchen window. Nature will provide a show during breakfast.

The shrubbery on the other side of the house, which we will walk by, is all arranged to appeal to the eye.

Finally, notice the arrangement of the walkways, the lawn furniture, all of it especially in relation to the large trees. A family will grow here. Children will play. Lovers will take walks. The ederly will sit and recall their lives. You see, the property itself is a stage, and I am setting it.

I hope this has helped. Yes, you too, and you're welcome. Please tell your teacher I said hello, and I will probably see you in the play next month. Goodbye now.

Monologue #2 Accountant

Hi. Welcome to the third floor, where we do the accounting. Did you have any trouble finding us? I didn't think you would.

There's a water fountain at the end of the hall and some cups. Why don't we stroll down there and get some to sip. This is a school project, right? You're supposed to find out how my theatre studies come up in my career? Is that about right?

There's a table in the main vestibule on this floor, plenty of light, and some comfortable chairs. A few people may pass through, but why don't we do the interview there? This way.

Okay, if you're comfortable, I'll start. My parents got me into acting at a local theatre when I was in elementary school. I was never the most expressive, but one knack I had was an ability to memorize lines. I liked doing it, and that got me some parts that were really above my acting skill level. They always knew they could rely on me to know the script.

I believe that acting developed the innate talent I had for memorization, and it is a talent I use in accounting all the time. I'll come back to that.

Accounting, you see, is keeping up with money and material assets. We make records of the money the company receives and the money it spends. We make catalogues of the stuff the company owns. We keep up with our debts, both that we owe and how much is owed to us. If something is missing or the numbers don't add up, our job is to find out why.

So as an accountant I am put in situations every day where I have to memorize things. I have to hold several facts in mind at once and know the relationships between them. Then I often have to recite the information to department heads and other accountants. I developed my memorization and confidence for this activity in theatre.

Something else I regularly have to do is make presentations. They can be done over computers or in person. They usually involve making visual displays of information so company executives can make spending decisions. Yes, pie charts, Venn Diagrams, and other type charts.

That may sound very cut and dry, but as so many great plays emphasize, we don't know the future. Even the most objective executive often has to work from hunches and feelings. So I make my presentations with feelings in mind... like a play. I have to point out areas where we need to improve and celebrate areas where we are doing well. I tell stories that involve math.

You may notice the way I am dressed-- business boring-- but part of this job is looking professional, and something I learned in theatre is that wardrobe is a third of telling us who the character is. At this facility, it is important that I look the part of an accountant.

An accounting office is a human place, and that always means some theatre.

You're welcome, and I am honored that you came by. Take the elevator on this end and you will be close to the visitor parking lot.

Monologue #3 HairDresser/Beautician/Cosmetologist

Yes, I'm the Hairdresser/Beautician/Cosmetologist. So you're the student who wants to interview me? My first customer will be here in about thirty minutes, and I need to sweep some hair clippings off the floor. I hope you don't mind. You can sit in the old hair dryer chair. Just raise the dome.

I had never given much thought to how my early participation in theatre connects to my career until your teacher contacted me about this interview, but as I thought about it, I realized there were several connections.

I took my first theatre course in high school. I was a shy person, but I needed an elective and art did not fit my schedule. My roles were small, but I excelled at helping my fellow students with makeup. Even as a small child I had always enjoyed dressing up and face paint. I like to look my best, and I like to see others look their best. I like the feeling of personal connection too.

But I realize that makeup is an obvious skill for a cosmetologist to recall from theatre. There are others that are not obvious. I do hair and makeup for weddings. A wedding is almost exactly like a play. Timing is important. Sometimes my work begins a full six hours prior to the beginning of the wedding itself.

I think of each bride as a masterpiece. Her appearance should be breath taking of course, but there are bridesmaids and grooms and groomsmen to consider too. I have to coordinate with the colors of the wedding. I take my cues from wedding directors. Once the process begins, there is no pausing, no turning back, and it's one the most special days in the lives of some people. It's exciting and exhausting, and no matter what happens, the show must go on.

Also, my shop here has some similarities to a theatre. There are rituals. When a customer arrives, I almost always wash their hair. That is not always necessary, but it puts the customer at ease. It's the opening act. It helps build a bond with the customer, and it sets the stage for the process that is to follow, which is kind of like a story. The story concludes when I spin them around to face the large mirror, and their hairstyle is complete. Would you believe I have seen people cry because of their transformation?

But I will tell you the most important theatre skill for a person like me. It's the social interaction that helps me combat my tendency to be shy. That's why one of my main social outlets to this day is in local theatre. I love the feeling of being a part of a production.

Well, it's almost time for me to turn my "open" sign around. I have enjoyed it. Here's my business card. Have a good day.

Monologue #4 Physician

Hi. Thanks for waiting on me. I hope you don't mind if I eat. That's why I invited you to meet here in a hospital cafeteria, Sorry. Also, I will try to go through this as quickly as I can.

You want to know about the skills I learned in theatre and how they apply to my work as a doctor, right?

I took theatre classes almost all the way through school, starting in elementary and going right up until my last year at college before going to Medical School. I often played a lead role.

"Bedside manner" is an old expression for the way a doctor relates to patients. For the doctor patient relationship to work well, there has to be trust. A doctor must have a stern but soothing mannerism, must convey compassion, must take time to really listen to each patient and sympathize with their pains.

I don't always feel up to playing the part of the sympathetic, caring physician. Sometimes I am going through problems in my personal life, and I have to force myself to concentrate and present myself to a patient as a professional. What would you call that if not theatre?

You could say that doctor visits, both when the patient visits my office, and I visit the patient in the hospital, are choreographed. There is an order in which it all happens. At my office, the patient first meets the receptionist, someone who we make sure is pleasant and understands basic etiquette. The receptionist is the usher of a theatre.

Then there are preliminary meetings with nurses. Not only is there practical value in this, like taking the patient's blood pressure, the meeting sets the tone. When the last nurse has finished asking questions and has outlined the patient's needs for me, she leaves the patient alone in a room, usually for a minute or two.

The interlude creates the atmosphere for my appearance. The patient is mindful of why they are there. At that point, I put all my personal issues aside and appear in the room in full, focused, doctor mode. It's not that I'm trying to be special, but it all works better this way. Done properly, it all falls into place like a play where everyone knows their parts.

Same is true of visits with patients in the hospital. Even if I am well acquainted with a patient's condition, I always take some records to look over. People need to see physical evidence that you are giving them due consideration. That's important. I never sit down in the room. I hover around the bed and often do traditional doctor things like listen to their heart or their breathing. Even if the patient isn't there for a lung or heart procedure, the contact and the personal attention is important. It is a form of theatre, really.

I am so sorry, but speaking of patients, my watch tells me it is time to go make some visits. I wish you the best with your studies.

Monologue #5

Computer Programmer

I picked this coffee shop because I actually do a lot of my work here. Let me get you a soda or how about an Italian Cream?

There ya go. So I'm supposed to tell you how my theatre studies have given me skills in the computer field? That will be easy, but really quick, did you know that the greatest thought leader in the computer field that ever lived attributed a lot of his success to studying calligraphy, which is writing with old fashioned fancy letters? It gave his company an edge in the field of graphics. His computers were programmed with beautiful typography while the others used block fonts. He said it made all the difference.

And that is exactly how the skills I gained in theatre help me in programming. We call the face of a computer a screen, same as we call the face of a television or the front part of a movie theater. Those mediums owe their existence to theatre. Many early movies in fact were just plays performed for the camera. For decades computers have become more and more visual. More and more we think of a computer as a place to express life and to communicate, not just do math.

So as I'm developing software I think of the computer screen as a window on the world, same as a stage is a window into a story. I stress to the team that I work with that we must always keep aesthetic considerations in mind.

If anyone doubts that computers tell stories, did you know that most police forces these days have at least one detective that specializes in constructing timelines of crimes based on the digital activities of victims and possible perpetrators?

Writing was always my favorite part of theatre classes. I learned a lot about structuring my thoughts. I learned how to break a story down into digestible pieces and to arrange it so the audience could interpret it. That relates in a big way to what I do with coding.

I use memorization skills, visualization skills, reading skills, writing skills, but maybe more importantly, the world of programming work is not some dry place devoid of human contact and interaction. Far from it. My team works close together, sometimes for hours at a time. Working together online actually intensifies our need for the kind of skills you learn in theatre. I have to project, to really put my ideas and sometimes even my feelings out there.

Finally, I'd like to show you some of the work that I am proudest of. It's outdated now, but it's a program I helped write for a restaurant chain to train their new servers. Notice how you see the cartoon faces. Notice how it is all framed. Notice the body language. The way I envisioned it and set it up goes back to the skills I learned in Theatre.

It was a pleasure to meet you. I hope this is what you needed. Have a nice afternoon.

Monologue #6 Guitar Player/Singer

I need to run upstairs and grab my guitar. There's a little amphitheatre in my family's backyard. Why don't you meet me back there? I'll bring some filtered water from my mom's refrigerator.

Here ya go. Now, I'm supposed to tell you how the stuff I learned in theatre comes up in my life as a working musician? Okay, gotcha. This is going to be really easy, ha ha. I've been involved with theatre and music my whole life.

Well first of all, music has always been directly associated with theatre. I've played in the pit for several musicals. I'm still in college, and the music department and the theatre department collaborate all the time. So that part of it is really obvious.

I'm not a traditional student, though, mind you. I'm going slowly, taking a class here and there. I'll eventually get a degree hopefully with a double major for when I'm older, you know something to fall back on, but for now I'm at an age and have a skill level where I can make a living and save money singing and playing.

I'm the most common kind of working musician. I play mostly covers in restaurants and nightclubs...

Cover? That's another way of saying I play popular songs that other people have made famous. Let's say you and your family are going out to dinner, and there are two restaurants that are about the same, but one has someone playing fun songs, the songs everyone knows and can sing along? Where are you gonna go? Unless you're planning to have some serious discussion over dinner, you're going to break for the fun atmosphere. Life can be pretty dull, and as an entertainer, I try to add some color and fun to it.

Playing and singing is about more than just getting in the right key and hitting the right notes. You have to sell the song by acting it out. That is theatre. You really have to let yourself feel each song as you sing it. Sometimes it's method acting.

But beyond the playing and singing, the most important thing you can have in this line of work is what they call "stage presence." It's your persona while you are performing, and it is theatrical. It's like you create a character. I'm dressed in that character right now. You see the holes in my jeans? You see this old hat? This worn out shirt? I never dressed like this growing up. I went to a prep school, and I bought this get up at a second hand store. Yeah, I'm playing the part of the traveling singer, poor in worldly goods but rich in song. My parents kinda hate it, but it's what the crowds like.

I brought my cover act guitar down here because it is a prop. I own four guitars. My classical guitar, which I use in the musician's pit for plays, is shiny and clean. So are the other two, with just a little wear, but the one I use when I play shows has stickers and writing, and is beat up and cracked. It's part of the image. It's a prop. I get completely into the character.

And that's how I use theatre skills as a working musician. Sure I'll pick out a song for you. What do you wanna hear?

Monologue #7 Tugboat Captain

Be careful there. Hold on to the railing. Keep going. Climb right up here. I believe the best way to give you the information you need will be to take you on a tour of my boat.

So you want to know which skills I learned in my school's theatre classes that have transferred to my profession as a tugboat captain? Let's proceed to the starboard side, and I'll tell you all about it.

You probably already know, but just to be clear, a tugboat pushes and pulls other vessels, usually in a harbor but it can be anywhere that extra power and control is needed.

First thing is, a captain on any vessel must have firm command. That is built on respect and trust, but all the respect in the world doesn't matter if you can't communicate clearly and authoritatively. My earliest experience talking to groups of people was in theatre. When I was in middle school, they had us doing a play set out west. I got picked to be the marshall, and I had to tell all the cowboys the way it was going to be, and I had to make them scared. I got applause for the way I launched into it.

But having command is more than just the way I talk, it's the way I carry myself, the way I show interest in my crew's concerns, my work ethic in general. This boat has a crew of fifteen, but we're never all on the boat at the same time. We rotate in and out. When I'm on shore, my first mate is in command. As officers we have a higher level of commitment to the boat, and it shows. As officers, you might say, we are playing roles. That doesn't mean that we are less than genuine. Quite the opposite. It means we let our most genuine and real commitment shine.

Now let's walk up to the bow. You see that big red ship across the harbor there? She's being loaded with cargo. We'll be taking her to sea tonight. It's an effort that will involve a bar pilot, a couple of navigators, two captains, and other officers and crew. Everyone must coordinate. Everyone must communicate. Everyone must play their part. See how the language of theatre flows right into it? But yes, it is like a play. That means timing, and timing is a skill that I developed in theatre.

Bringing two ships together is a kind of dance, like the two main characters in a musical maneuvering their way through struggles. It has to be done gently. There are steps. There are obstacles, but if we do it right, it all works out in the end. I learned a lot about dancing… and the way characters find their way to be together... in my theatre classes.

I never directed a play, but I learned a lot from watching the director, and it applies to my profession. Our high school director would walk around and observe us from different angles, always seeing things from the bigger perspective, always thinking about how it all works together. If I had gone into theatre, I believe I would have naturally gravitated to directing. I tend to see the big picture. It's the skill of seeing the big picture that enabled me to become a captain.

You're welcome. Be careful there. Hold onto the railing. Fair winds.

Monologue #8 Hotel Manager

Hi, come on in. I'll be right out. I'll meet you at the far table in the lobby. How about a bottled water?

We are busy today. We're at full capacity. Fortunately I've got a full staff and they can handle things. It feels good to get off my feet for a few minutes.

Now, I believe your teacher told me that I'm supposed to tell you how studying theatre gave me some skills for my job.

Good question. My major in college was hospitality management, which is more or less the same as hotel management, but it goes into the depths of resort hotels, cruise ships, and ski lodges. We study food preparation, recreation, and even spa treatments. It's far more extensive than what you would associate with the overnight hotels you find along the highway. I always have had a lot of energy and enjoyed a fast pace so it only made sense that I minored in theatre and danced in a couple of musicals in college.

Right off the top I can tell you that this hotel has an entertainment component. We have a restaurant on the top floor with regularly scheduled piano players, a ballroom where events of many kinds are held including dancing, and a small lounge that faces the street. We have music and comedians in the lounge.

All the performing arts flow into theatre and have a theatrical element. I may have a pianist apply who is really good, but they have to understand the aesthetic of our restaurant. Our pianists are required to dress at the black tie level. They have to look the part. I gained my basic understanding of performance aesthetics in theatre.

Most of our guests at any given moment are regular business travelers. We have a point system that rewards them for loyalty so it's really about building and maintaining a relationship with each guest. Their life away from home can be lonely, and they need to be able to make quick, friendly connections. So our bartenders are trained not just to serve beverages but to be as friendly as possible, to get to know guests and to introduce them to each other. You could compare it to improv. I learned improv in theatre, and I insist that my bartenders be able to think on their feet.

In this industry, we have to be conscious of our guests the way actors are conscious of their audience. We have our break room for down time. It's like being backstage. Sometimes we deal with difficult guests and sometimes we have plenty to complain about to each other, but when we are in sight of the customers, we play our parts cheerfully as bellhops, clerks, pool attendants, or whatever our role is.

As a manager of a physical facility, I feel like I learned a lot from the stage managers I got to observe in my theatre studies. They had a foot both in the fantasy world of the play and the real world, usually had a lot of energy and made quick decisions, and they were always putting out little fires, solving one problem after another. I felt drawn to that kind of challenge.

You're welcome. Tell your teacher I said hello. We were classmates, you know.

Monologue #9 Automobile Salesperson

Well, hello there! Glad to have you here. We have a great selection of used cars with easy financing, and the best prices in the region. Like our ad says on TV, we'll make you a deal that'll feel unreal. Ha ha!

No down payment if you qualify, and if you don't, well, we'll take it off the front end and put it on the back end and get you behind the wheel today!

Oh? You're the student here for the interview? Oh, I'm sorry. It's nice to meet you. I hope you don't mind that we do the interview here in the lot, ya know, if a customer pulls up, I like to greet them the way I just greeted you.

And since you're here to find out how my theatre skills come into my work life, well, you've already had a sample. Sales is a performance art! I started learning acting in school, but some of the old sales guys taught me a lot too, and the funny thing about acting is, the better you are at it, the less you are acting. It's like summoning some real part of yourself.

One older salesperson, who you used to work here, had an accent like a character from a western movie, talked real slow, but it was like he would put his customers in a trance.

But I also learned something from writing. We often had to write scenes in class. Well, As I get to know each potential customer, I try to find out what they envision themselves doing in the car and suggest to them a vision of their life at its best in the car. Let's say I'm trying to sell a luxury car to a lawyer. I mention the climate control, the comfortable leather seats. I try to get the lawyer to form a picture of arriving at court relaxed and refreshed and ready to present evidence.

Let's say I'm trying to sell a van to a traveling musician. I emphasize space for instruments and electronic equipment, and maybe even enough space to sleep over night.

Let's say I'm trying to sell a truck to a farmer. It's all about power and versatility. In other words, I have to get my customers to see themselves using the vehicle and it meeting their expectations. I am helping them write the story of their life in the vehicle.

Believe it or not, I am not a natural when it comes to speaking out. I've had to work to develop that, and my theatre classes helped with that in a big way. One of our teachers had us write monologues and deliver them, and that was a very helpful exercise over all. I am a better communicator for it.

And one other thing I learned is that every minor detail matters. If I hesitate while talking about a car, even a moment's hesitation gets judged and interpreted. People watch each other pretty closely.

Well, I hope this was what you needed. Here's my card when you're ready for a set of wheels. Good afternoon!

Monologue #10 Event Promoter

Is this the first time you've been in a radio station? Ah well, you're in for a show. My favorite thing is when I'm having a conversation with a DJ. They'll be talking with you one second, then they ask you to hold on, they go on the air, come back off and pick up the conversation like they never skipped a beat.

I know that I'm supposed to tell you how the skills I learned in theatre are part of the work I do, and since I'm an event promoter, a lot of that should be obvious, but I want to talk about some of it that's not so obvious. Event promotion sounds like endless fun. I mean who wouldn't want to spend their time planning concerts and sports tournaments? The fact is, the business side of it can be pretty dry, still that's the part where I think you can find the practical skills.

One of the biggest parts of this job is negotiation. Let's say I'm working on a music festival, and I'm responsible for bringing in five acts. That means I have to be in contact with all their booking agents. Can you get me this singer on the 8th? No? How about this band on the 9th? Okay, I'm penciling them in. How about this guitar player on the 8th? After we figure out who I can get, we figure out if they are going to do one set or two sets, and how much they get paid. It's a lot of back and forth, and sometimes it changes at the very last second. Once I've secured the acts, then I have to deal with managers. They're the ones who oversee the day to day operations of the musical acts. It can get really strange. An act may insist that the dressing room backstage have fresh fruit and lemonade... or maybe a bucket of bubble gum. You never know.

Negotiation is largely a matter of acting and reading through the acting that others are trying to put over on you. Acting games helped me develop these skills.

Part of what I do is pretty much the same as casting. Let's say I'm organizing a tournament at a minor country club. I would not be able to bring in any big name golfers so here's the alternative. I bring in retired athletes from other sports. Some people enjoy seeing their old football heroes for example. Knowing who fits where is the key.

That brings me around to a skill that is a little more obvious, and the reason I wanted to meet you here at this radio station. I'm going to record a commercial for an upcoming concert. I could hire someone else to do it, but it was my skill making these type commercials that got me interested in promotions in the first place. You can watch me through the glass when I go into the booth. You may think it's silly, but you will see body language to go along with my enthusiasm for the show.

It is acting, but it is real. I mean, I really do love the shows that I put together. I want everyone to have a good time. I want everyone to see the show.

I'm going to make several of these, then I have editing. You can show yourself out when you get tired of watching.

Monologue #11 Basketball Coach

Hey, come on in. The gym is kinda warm. So your theatre teacher sent you over to talk about how my theatre studies play a role in my work as a coach?

It would probably be easier to list the areas of coaching basketball that do not involve theatre in some way. The fact is a sport played for an audience is theatre. It is a form of entertainment. A game is a play with an uncertain outcome.

The structure of a sport assigns a role to a coach. What I mean by that is you will notice that the team sits in a certain area during a game, and it is the coach's role, and usually there are rules dictating it, that the coach must remain in that area. In other words, what I do during a game is for audience consumption. It's part of the drama. Some coaches play it very stern and unemotional. Others shout and stand up and wave their arms and point. Me? Well, I guess I'm somewhere in the middle when it comes to the way I act during games.

There are other theatrical things too… like meeting the opposing coach before a game and shaking hands, also meeting again after the game as a display of sportsmanship. One of my least favorite theatrical things is interviews with reporters. There is only so much that a coach can say about a team's performance. It all comes down to "we need to score more points than the other team" and either we did or didn't. So sometimes you say things like "We need to improve at our passing game" or "we need to improve on defense" but it's all just jargon really.

Then there is the theatrical aspect of teaching players and motivating them. When I'm teaching the fundamentals of the game and working with players on their skills, I sound a lot like any other teacher. I'm mainly trying to communicate sincerely and effectively. My background in theatre helped me with projection so that is a skill I use. At other times, my message to the team is really not so much about any particular point, it's to get them in the right emotional and mental state. I may yell, I may tell an exciting story. I may tell them how great they are. I may tell them how not so great they are. Whatever works to get them ready for the challenge, to get their adrenaline flowing. This is usually before games and during half time. I've never been one to deliver verbal beat downs. That is never necessary, and it doesn't work.

Before a game, the players warm up, and this is important for getting in the other team's head. There is a theatrical element in it. You want the other team to be intimidated. So that's when you want your guys to dunk the ball a few times, make some fancy shots and passes. There's so much ritual, and it's all theatre. The announcer calls out each player's name, one at a time. This is to get the teams and the audience excited. Usually there is music. The cheerleaders perform stunts and gymnastics to get the crowd excited.

So as I coach I play a role in a theatrical event every time we play a game. There are few theatre skills that I don't use.

I hope this is what you needed. You have your hall pass, right?

Monologue #12 Graphics Artist

Come on in. Sorry for the clutter, but we are a busy advertising agency. So you have an assignment to find out how studying theatre contributed skills to my job?

My mom had me in plays before I can even remember. My family was really into theatre. I studied theatre throughout my school years and into college.

I was always artistic, and one practical application of artistic talent that is in demand is graphics art. Graphics art has mostly to do with the design of words on paper or on a screen, but it takes in other kinds of art as well. Sometimes I make my own illustrations sometimes I use the work of others.

My involvement in theatre taught me to frame things, to see things the way an audience sees them. So let's say I'm doing some work for a grocery store that is running a big sale on Thanksgiving food. The way I lay the page out I put the spotlight on those foods. And of course it's good to know the traditions associated with Thanksgiving, most of which were communicated to me in plays.

Take a look at what I am working on right now. My agency has been hired by a dentist's office that is new to the area and trying to let the community know that it's here. On the front, you see this happy family, all with big smiles? That is what they call a stock photo-- which means a random photo from a site on the internet. I just copied and pasted it into this document. No, they're not customers. They probably don't even live around here. Yeah, they have really nice teeth, don't they? And that's the point they are illustrating. That's the story they are telling. Use this dentist, get nice teeth, have a happy family.
But something I learned in my theatre studies is that a great playwright shows more than they tell. It's all about letting the audience work off their own interpretations and assumptions. A graphics artist does the same thing. If we communicate correctly, whoever views our work feels it in their subconscious. A big bold letter screams, a small curley letter whispers.

I think I knew that I was destined to go into graphics art in highschool. Of all the things we were each allowed to contribute to school productions of plays, my favorite was to work with the printed material. I loved to help design the flyers and programs, especially the programs. A well designed program for a play is a thing of beauty, something to save, and if you're playing the role of your dreams, maybe even something to treasure.

The written word is the blueprint for the spoken word of a play. A skill that working in theatre has given me is that as I produce the written word I am keenly aware of how it will ultimately sound. Many readers always translate printed words into sound, you know.

But most importantly, theatre developed my imagination, and imagination is the most important skill a graphics artist can have.

I hope I have answered your questions. Have a nice day.

Monologue #13 Sales Account Manager

Hi, I realize a fastener sales office is a strange place to meet, but we are happy to have you here. Nothing more exciting than fastener sales. Ha ha. I joke! Ha ha.

I took a couple of theatre classes in high school. I liked theatre so much I took a couple more in college as electives. My major was marketing, but I use my theatre skills all the time. In fact, I'm using them right now, ha ha.

I need to be specific and tell you what I sell. I sell industrial grade steel fasteners, mainly nuts and bolts. But there are various kinds of clamps and even some rivets. Let's say there's a cement company building a new mixer and an engineer designs some stairs for workers to climb to the top of it. They are going to use metal support beams and sheet metal, and they're going to have to hold it all together. That's where I come in. They give me a call, and I help them find exactly what they need. I even advise them on issues like safety.

But the main part of the job is the smallest part of the job in this realm of sales. It is mainly about knowing and being known to the engineers and other decision makers. My company gives me a daily amount of money to spend on dinners with decision makers, golf with decision makers, even entertainment like going to a play after work. Each decision maker's company has an account with us. You could call me the fastener, ha ha. I maintain the relationship that maintains the account. It's mostly about being chummy with the decision makers.

Sometimes it's easy to pal around with a decision maker. Other times, not so much. Sometimes I have to pretend to be interested in a boring story as a decision maker is telling it. Sometimes I have to pretend to laugh at a joke that I don't really find funny. I have to be polite at all times. I have to stay positive nearly all the time. The one goal is to keep our company on their mind so that when they need fasteners they will come to us without giving it much thought. I have to convince them that we are good and honest people to deal with.

What I've told you is just the basics. I have to be able to study characters to know how best to relate to them. That means knowing motivations. Is a customer motivated by time factors and they want their fasteners now! Or are they more motivated by getting just the right fasteners? That is a skill from theatre. I have to be able to really express myself, again a theatre skill.

Now you're probably asking why I said earlier that I am using my theatre skills right now? I will tell you that I am putting my best foot forward. That doesn't mean that I'm being fake. It just means that I'm on my best behavior. It means that I'm careful with what words I say. I am to some degree performing a part.

But then… so are you… Have a nice afternoon.

Monologue #14 Technical Writer

Hi. This is a lovely coffee shop, isn't it? It's where I do about half my work. Would you like a soda?

Now I'm supposed to tell you about the skills I learned in theatre and how they come into play in my occupation, right?

First off, my occupation is that of a technical writer. Have you ever got a new phone and it had a book of instructions? That kind of writing is called technical writing. Technical writing is used in many industries. Let's say an engineer designs a building and wants to write some things down so that the building contractor will better understand how to construct it. A technical writer would help with that. It is different from creative writing in that you have to be very precise, very exact. When you're doing technical writing, you want to find the words that work perfectly. Also a certain amount of math comes into it.

I took theatre classes in middle school. Unfortunately my highschool did not have a theatre program, but I minored in theatre in college. My major was English. I later took a few more courses to prepare myself for a technical writing job. I currently work with a company that manufactures maritime communications products such as the radio you might find on a tugboat.

It would be my job to discover what each knob and switch do. I would need to know what the numbers on the screen mean. I would have to understand every aspect of how to operate the radio and then communicate that to the officers and crew of the vessels that will be using the radio. There is usually a printed pamphlet but now it is common for the instructions to be saved on the internet so that they can be retrieved anywhere at any time.

When you think about it, this is script writing. It is telling a story. The reader is learning a script to be acted out. I have to visualize the same as a playwright. I have to tell the story in a linear and precise manner, but it is still storytelling.

Another thing I learned in theatre was how to work in a group. Theatre is a collaborative effort. As a technical writer, I have to work with illustrators and match my writing to their drawings. I have to work with graphics artists who bring mechanical illustrations together. I have to work with editors who notice flaws and help fix them. The designers of the product are the most important people I work with. They are my muses so to speak.

Then finally, to see if we have done our job properly, our company gets someone who knows nothing about the product to attempt to operate it using what the team has put together. That is like the opening night of a play. They video the process in case there are difficulties. If all goes well, it is like a successful opening night. We have ourselves a small celebration because sometimes one technical manual can represent a year of work, maybe even more.

It's been a pleasure to meet you.

Monologue #15 Postal Worker

Hi. I hope you don't mind that I parked here in your driveway. I will take a few minutes off of my route for this interview. It's okay, I was a little bit ahead of schedule.

I see you made us some lemonade. Perfect. The sun is really nice today, and this front porch is a good spot to soak it up.

I took theatre in highschool. I got a job with the post office right after I graduated. I deliver mail on a route here in the suburbs. It's a pleasant job for the most part, and I certainly do use some of the skills I learned in theatre.

I will start with the fact that as a mail carrier I wear a uniform. I could easily remove the hat or change into a tee shirt on the road, but the uniform is important. We learned the importance of wardrobe in theatre. People make snap judgments about who we are. If I'm walking into someone's yard, and they don't know who I am, that could cause fear on their part. You never know how they might react. If I'm in full uniform, holding a parcel in my hands with a big address sticker on it, they know immediately who I am.

At the beginning of each shift, I arrange all the mail in order by address. This is my script for the day. It's what I have to do. It's usually busiest around the holidays. Speaking of which, I often receive little gifts in the mailbox at that time. It's usually just cookies or maybe an ornament of some kind, but it means a lot. It really helps with feeling the human element, and in a real way that is theatre. Most of the meaning is in the gesture itself, you see, and it works both ways. If I see mail start to pile up, especially in the box of an elderly recipient, I check on them. I ask around the community to find out what the situation is. If things don't look good, I may call the county to send a social worker out. If I do my job mindfully, it is so much more than just someone putting letters in boxes. I become an integral part of the community.

Another skill that theatre developed was visualization. That helps me in the hours I spend driving. My radio is my main company out here on the road. I listen to a great variety of programming. I enjoy news shows, talk shows, sports broadcasts, radio plays on public radio, and different kinds of music. Sometimes I listen to podcasts, but mainly I listen to radio. Well, it all takes place in the theatre of the mind. I visualize it happening. If I'm listening to a basketball game, and I hear the excitement in the commentators voice, I can see the ball dropping into the basket or a blocked pass. It's a wonderful mental exercise that I really enjoy.

I appreciate your interest. Now I have to deliver the rest of today's mail. Oh here is a letter for you.

Monologue #16 Flight Attendant

Welcome to the airport. My flight departs in about an hour so I have some time. Plus it's good to get off my feet.

So I'm going to be telling you how theatre studies gave me practical skills for my work as a flight attendant.

I should tell you first of all that the primary job of a flight attendant is not what the public thinks. It's not about getting people pillows and blankets or bringing them their dinner, at least not primarily. A flight attendant's primary job is to maintain an atmosphere of calmness with the passengers. It's all about crowd control. We get a lot of focused training in that and we are always learning new techniques.

One of the first things that happened on my path to becoming a flight attendant was I got certified in CPR and first aid. If someone is having a medical emergency, I have to know the first things to do so that at a bare minimum I stabilize them until the plane can land and they can get help from professional emergency personnel.

So that's my real job, keep the passengers calm no matter the situation, and now the theatre skills. Emotions are contagious. We learned that in theatre. We learned methods to summon our emotions. Being able to tap into the right emotion at the right time and to control it, that's what makes a good actor, and that is exactly the same thing that makes a good flight attendant. Let's say we are going through some turbulence. The plane is rocking and shaking a little. Even if I'm scared, I can't let the passengers know it. I have to convey a peaceful feeling at all times.

At the beginning of each flight, flight attendants act out what to do in emergency situations. We show passengers how to use the emergency oxygen supply and the flotation devices.

Then there are all the rituals of serving food and drinks that are no different from wait staff in any restaurant. There is an element of theatre in that.

The most severe emergency situation I ever faced on a flight was an elderly woman having chest pains. One of my fellow flight attendants got her some medicine. We moved her to an area on the plane out of sight of the rest of the passengers. As my friend held her hand and the pilot re-routed to the closest airport and got Emergency Response prepared for the landing, I spoke to the passengers. I calmed myself, took a deep breath, and said, "Because one of our passengers has some medical concerns, we will be making a brief landing that is not on our flight schedule. Be sure to clear the aisle. Please fasten your seatbelts, put your seats in an upright position and remain seated until further notice. Thank you for your cooperation."

I can tell you without any doubt that performing memorized lines on stage in school did a lot toward preparing me for that. You have to be able to overcome the pressure. You have to maintain inner balance.

It will soon be time to start boarding. Nice to meet you.

Monologue #17 Police Officer

They make a good omelette here, and I get a discount for being a police officer in uniform. That means discount security for their diner, which is fine by me.

Your teacher says I'm supposed to tell you about how taking theatre classes helped develop some of the skills I have to use as a police officer. I put some thought into it last night. I was surprised at how much it comes into play.

The very first thing that comes to mind is something we are trained in extensively at the police academy, and we practice it our entire career. It is called "command presence." Let's say that I'm pulling someone over for a speeding ticket. I can't just casually stroll up to their car and smile awkwardly. I have to walk with purpose. I have to walk standing straight up like someone with authority because in that situation I have authority.

In a situation like that even good people will sometimes start talking nervously, start asking me questions, start making excuses trying to get out of a speeding ticket. I can't let that affect me. I have to be firm. I have to speak with a strong voice. I can't be rude, but I have to let them know they can't push me around. Any sign of weakness or uncertainty and they will pounce on it.

Command presence can be hard to maintain with common violators of traffic laws, but with really hardened criminals it is three times as hard. Sometimes they will literally fight you.

That brings me to another skill that I worked on in theatre, and that's physical acting. I used to love doing falls and sword fighting. I was always athletic so it was really my favorite part, and my teachers said I was good at it. Just knowing how to fall without getting hurt has come in handy a couple of times in police work.

One night I pulled a car over, and a big guy got out and pushed me. I knew it was too late to resist the momentum of the push, so I rolled down an embankment but I didn't get hurt, and I came right back up and arrested him.

Another major part of police work is testifying in court. The things that someone says at the time of an arrest are vital. The detectives use my word to build their case. I have to be able to recite the details of every case I'm involved with, and I have to do it without notes. It has to be from memory. That's what it means to testify. I have to memorize details like what a person was wearing when I saw them, how tall they were, things they said. It really can be a lot. Defense attorneys will try to find fault in my story, try to break me down. So I really have to be precise. I also have to deliver it all in such a way that a jury will take it seriously.

So yeah, there are several important skills from theatre that a police officer needs. I hope I've helped you. Now I've got to get back on my beat.

Monologue #18 Fruit and Vegetable Department Manager

Hi. I never thought I'd be giving an interview in a grocery store, but here you are. As I understand what your teacher asked, I'm supposed to tell you about how skills I learned in theatre come up in my job.

I had a lot of theatre involvement growing up. My parents had me in plays very young, and I took every theatre class in high school.

Why don't we start here with the bananas? Bananas are the most popular fruit. You could compare bananas to the lead role in a play. So they are front and center and have a display table completely to themselves. You might think of the display table the same as you would a stage.

Apples are our second most popular fruit. They also get their own display table. One thing I have to do is spray the fruit, just to make sure it glistens. When customers are walking by, the fruit really needs to grab their attention. We learned a lot about that sort of thing, especially working on costumes and promotions.

The vegetable area is a little less exciting than the fruit area. I think of the veggies as playing support roles, but really they are where the nutrition is. They are the foundation of a healthy diet. Still, it is all meant to catch the eye. Look at how the corn is stacked in these baskets. The baskets overflow with the corn, as if it is calling out to the customer to be chosen.

That brings up another area where theatre skills come in pretty handy, and it's dealing with customers. Someone may come in looking for black eyed peas, but all we have is purple hull peas. It's my job to make the customer feel better in a situation like that. I may tell them that we have black eyed peas coming in on the next truck, or I may tell them that the purple hulls are really fresh.

Whenever we offer discounts, I write it on these small chalkboards that I set up by whatever we are discounting. I like to add stars and exclamation points. I've even been known to draw funny cartoon versions of the fruit, ya know, give the fruit little faces. Anything to bring a smile or a good feeling here in the fruit and vegetable department.

Growing up I was always kind of introverted. I was never very outgoing by nature, but theatre helped me with that. If I am stacking grapefruit, and a customer walks by, I tell them hello and welcome them to the store. I ask them if I can help them find anything. I may offer them a compliment on their haircut or shoes. My theatre classes helped me learn to communicate more, to reach out more. It's a good skill to have. I use it every day. You're welcome. It has been enjoyable meeting you. Do you like cantaloupe? I need to make room for a new shipment of cantaloupe, and I have two left over. Why don't you take one of them, free of charge.

Monologue #19 Veterinary Assistant

So you're the student I am supposed to be giving an interview? I hope you don't mind a little barking in the background, but this is a veterinary clinic. I wish I could take you in the back and show you some of what we do, but the lobby will have to do. The Vet sends greetings by the way.

I've known your teacher for many a year. We took theatre together. If I understand, I am supposed to tell you about the skills I learned in theatre that I use in my career.

I guess I will start by telling you about my career. I love animals. I always had a strong inclination to work with animals. I considered pursuing Vet school, but a veterinarian puts in as much school as a doctor for humans. That can be socially isolating and I am a very social person. Because there is a business aspect of their work, it is not unusual for a vet to work sixty hours a week. I wanted to settle down and start a family so I pursued an associate's degree to become a Vet assistant.

The most obvious way I use my studies in theatre is in handling animals. Animals respond in a big way to body language. Body language is how animals communicate with each other, and we have to be able to speak it. I learned a lot about it doing physical theatre.

Let's say there is a dog that is prone to biting. Without hurting the dog, there are techniques for communicating dominance. Once the dog knows that it is not in charge, and that I am thoroughly in charge, it will instinctively relax and go along with whatever I am trying to do. Once the dog accepts my authority, I then need to communicate friendliness by patting and rubbing in a relaxing way.

You might say the way we take in our patients and relate to their owners is scripted. There are procedures we have to memorize and follow. I then have to relate information to the Vet. My theatre classes certainly helped improve my verbal communication skills.

But maybe the most important of the skills I worked on in theatre that I use as a veterinary assistant is relating to people with feeling. I remember one of my teachers saying that the way two actors relate to each other was like a game of tennis. Each actor had to react to the other actor, and the reactions were to go back and forth, usually with escalation like a game of tennis.

Pets are so important to people on an emotional level, and sometimes people are very upset when they bring them in. Sometimes they may see their beloved pet for the final time right here in this lobby. It is heartbreaking. Sometimes I break down and cry with them. I do my best to reassure them that their pet will not experience any pain.

I feel honored that you wanted to know about my career. If you ever need a pet, I would remind you to please adopt one from a shelter. Please tell my old friend, your teacher, that I say hello.

Monologue #20 Carpenter

Hi. Welcome to this home construction site. One of your classmates was here a couple of days ago interviewing the landscaper. Put this hard hat on. We're going to walk around a little bit.

As I understand it I am supposed to tell you how I learned some skills in theatre that I now use in my work as a carpenter. Okay, well, first of all, there are different kinds of carpenters that specialize in different kinds of construction and repair. I do two types of carpentry, frame and cabinet. For this job I've been contracted to do both.

I took theatre for most of my years in school, and I just sorta fell into the technical side. I especially liked building sets and props. My dad was a carpenter, and I was already learning how to work wood around his shop so it came naturally to me. Not only did building props give me practice at the basics of carpentry, it really helped me develop my creative sense about things. I was always having to think about how it all looked to the audience.

Building a house is a lot like performing a play, and by that I mean the day to day process of working from a blueprint and interacting with the other trades.

A blueprint is to a building what a script is to a play. Not only is there a visual depiction of what the building is going to look like, there are notes about the building process. You know how sometimes in a play, something will come up at the beginning in a small way, but then later after it has been forgotten it comes up in a big way?

The first team to work on a building or a house gets the ground ready. But you'll be surprised at who works next-- it's the plumbers. They come in and lay pipe in the ground. You'll see pipes sticking up everywhere. Then the concrete crew comes in and gets the foundation ready. Then the frame carpenters come in and build the structure. Then the roofers come and put the roof on so the wood doesn't get rained on. Then the plumbers come back and run pipe through the walls and the electricians run wires. Then lots of finishing work takes place, then the cabinetry. Then the plumbers come back and install the sinks and what have you. Finally the electricians make one more round to install electrical lighting and appliances. It can vary a little but that's the basics. It's been done on video, and you can watch it all in fast motion. It's quite a show.

The general contractor oversees the entire process and is the director. An inspector that comes out to make sure we do everything right is the same as a dramaturg. The people that are going to live in the house are the audience. Some will appreciate the work that went into the house. Some won't, but we want them all to enjoy their home.

I see my lunch break is almost over, and my crew is waiting. I enjoyed talking to you. I hope I gave you the information you need.

Monologue #21 Bus Driver

Come on board. I saved you the front seat. One time I was witness to a traffic accident and had to give an interview to a police officer this same way, over my shoulder. I hope you don't mind.

As I understand, I am going to tell you about the skills I learned from theatre that I use as a bus driver. I've had time to think it over, and I'll be happy to tell you all about it, but first, I need to make an announcement over the bus's PA system, "Next stop is Maple Street All passengers for the Maple Street Bus stop, be ready to exit in about one minute."

My involvement with theatre was mostly patchy growing up, a class here, a play there. I did a couple of plays in civic organizations, that kind of thing, but theatre was definitely part of my life. I mostly played supporting roles and comic roles.

I attended junior college but I never picked a major. It's not that I was lazy. Quite the opposite. I was so interested in so many subjects that I could not narrow it down. Rather than start in a four year school, I decided to get my commercial driver's license, which only took a couple of months, and I got into bus driving. The pay isn't bad. I see a great diversity of things, and I get to explore life. I even get to act in plays in community theatre. I am a people person by nature so it fits.

Excuse me, "We are at the Maple Street Stop. Passengers bound for Maple Street, please make your way to the front and exit carefully. Thank you for riding City Bus Line"

Communication, really being able to project, is the first skill that popped into my mind as I thought about the subject. I was never shy, but I remember a couple of directors encouraging me to really project my voice and to be quick about it, especially in the comic roles. There's timing involved with it, and I use that throughout the day as a bus driver. As you just saw, I am in constant communication with my passengers. I have to be crisp and clear and fast with my communication

Another skill I developed in theatre was memorization. I have to memorize my routes as a driver, and really know them. The traffic is different on every road I travel. I have to know what is where. Passengers are always asking me where different things are, where to shop, where to eat, where the post office is located. I consider it part of my job to be able to tell them. Electronics only goes so far in life. It's good to have real knowledge of the areas I work.

But the more I think about it, I guess the most important skill is just knowing how to work with people. Each passenger is acting out their script for the day, running their errands, going to see friends, coming home from work, and I have to be able to play my role. I work well with people. Theatre helped develop that skill.

I believe we're almost at your stop now. I've enjoyed the interview. Let me announce it to the passengers. "Broad Street stop is coming up in about one minute."

Monologue #22 Health Inspector

Hi, come on in. I can tell you authoritatively this is the cleanest diner in town. They always get the highest score, and they make a pretty good milkshake.

I have to admit I'm a little surprised that your teacher asked me to do this interview. I took a few theatre courses growing up and only one in college, and this is a science job that I do. I gave it some thought, though, and I believe I did learn some skills in theatre that come into this line of work.

So let me tell you about what I do. I work for the county health board. My job is to go from restaurant to restaurant and inspect to make sure that they are clean and that the food is safe to eat and prepared the right way.

To do that, I take samples and use chemical tests. That part of my job is very cut and dry. It's science. But there is another side of my job.

If restaurant owners disagree with me about a grade, they are apt to argue with me, and that arguing is always dramatic, "But we just cleaned that stove! That cutting area is only dirty because we just got a big order. It's usually not like that. Can't you give us a few minutes to get it clean again? My main employee is sick. Don't you understand? Why can't you just relax for once?"

On and on they go sometimes, and so a skill that I learned, at least indirectly, is how to be on the lookout for theatricality. When someone is protesting a little too much, what does that tell me? Everyone is an actor in some way or another. We all need to be aware of it. That's a skill.

But what about myself as an actor? Ha ha, well, there is that too. I've been offered bribes, usually in the form of free dinners. Restaurateurs have tried to find my weaknesses, believe me. So it is important for me to play my part, so to speak. I have to be bold. I have to be firm. I simply cannot allow myself to be pushed around. I cannot break character because if I do it once, my authority with the restaurant in question will be lost forever. Plus word gets around.

Finally, another skill I learned is to look beyond the surface of things to figure out the true story. There was a restaurant where other health inspectors were giving high scores. I don't think they were doing their inspections completely because the restaurant was upscale and everything was shiny and looked perfect. I made myself be thorough, and I found some shiny areas that had high levels of bacteria. If theatre teaches us anything it is to be aware that things are rarely what they first appear to be.

I know that my job isn't the most theatrical in the world, but still, there are definitely some skills that transfer. I hope what I have given you helps. Tell your teacher I said hello, and I hope you enjoy that milkshake.

Monologue #23 Personal Assistant

Hi, welcome to our office complex. I am sure your teacher told you that I am the personal assistant to the president of operations of a regional retail chain. We specialize in what we like to call tasteful, casual shoes and clothing.

The president's job is to oversee every aspect of the day to day business of the chain, from getting the floors polished to stocking the shelves to getting the lightbulbs changed in the restrooms. There are middle managers all up and down the line, but ultimately, it all has to come across the president's desk and get reported to the accounting department.

I have to be the eyes, ears, hands, and even the mouth of the president. Here's an example. Let's say that according to an accounting report, sales in the shoe department at store number eight are in serious decline. The president has me contact the human resources department to see if the decline coincides with changes in personnel. Let's say that the decline started when a new department manager was hired. The president would have me contact the store manager who would then either fire or demote the shoe department manager. Meanwhile the president would move on to solving other problems as I took care of the communication

Here is where my theatre skills, which I learned in high school and college, come into this. I have to be a projection of the president of the company. I often have to convey messages with a touch of the president's authority. And you know what? It's a hard role to play!

I have to surrender most of my feelings about the various situations and decisions the president makes and attempt to channel the president's feelings. Sometimes that really takes acting skills on my part.

Another aspect of this job is that I serve as a living prop, especially when the president is negotiating with the executives of other companies. I am the leader of the president's entourage. A part of what we do is make the president look important by catering to them. Again, that is not always a very easy job.

Why do I do it? Because one day I want to be an executive. I'm about to start work on an MBA in the fall, and I need this kind of experience. I need to get my own name out there.

Those other executives in those other companies, they will remember who I am. I play my part with great seriousness, you see.

One other skill that I would mention is script writing. We did many script writing exercises in my theatre classes. I arrange the president's travel schedule including flights, auto rental, hotels, dining, even some entertainment. I have to calculate the timing of it all, I have to plan it out and write it out.

Then I accompany the president on business travels and smooth out every process. For example, I will go to a hotel dining room and secure a table and order the food so that it is ready and waiting when the president arrives. You could call it direting.

You're welcome, and thank you for stopping by.

Monologue #24 Human Resources Manager

Hi, welcome to the office wing of the largest resort hotel on the river. We have a staff of over three hundred full time employees.

I have to tell you, it feels a bit strange to be giving an interview. Ordinarily I am the one conducting the interviews. My job as a Human Resource Manager is to serve as the face of the company to the individual employee and vice versa. Whenever someone is hired, they process through this office. That starts with an interview, right here in this room. This office also keeps records of employee performance. It physically distributes checks or statements of direct deposit to employees. When an employee is no longer with the company, we process them out of the system. If an employee has complaints, this is where they are invited to bring them. We also have to have expertise in employment laws and make sure that the company keeps those laws.

So what you're wanting to know is how the skills I learned in theatre come up in this profession?

I was heavily involved with the production of plays in college. They were fully produced by students, and in my junior and senior years, I worked in casting. That is a lot like what I do in the hiring process. Sometimes it is pretty straightforward. Someone applies for a specific job, and they get that job, but sometimes someone is looking for any work, and I have to decide where they fit best. For example, I might have to decide whether an applicant would make a better swimming pool attendant or a better groundskeeper. Their interview would be a lot like an audition. I do my best to get a sense of who they are, what they can do, and how best the company can use their skills.

Conducting the interview means being the face of the company, and that means professionalism. I have to let them know that although guests come here to relax and have fun, we still take our work very seriously. I have to give them some exposure to the atmosphere that we maintain and see how they respond to it.

I then introduce the potential employee to the head of the department where we agree they will fit best. The department head then conducts another interview. If all goes well, the department head gives me the greenlight to hire the applicant.

Hiring, you might say, is a scripted process, some of it is mandated by law. Employees have to be given a clear description of their job, who they answer to, the general rules of the hotel, and their legal rights as employees. We have to check their references and get medical clearances. We have to run background checks and provide uniforms. It's quite a process, but when we do it right it's like a play where everyone knows their lines.

If an employee files a complaint then I am the channel of communication to the company. I try to resolve these matters in a peaceful, timely manner. Working on a deadline to produce plays helped me gain skills I use all the time, especially where communication is concerned.

You're welcome. I enjoyed having you, and if you ever need a job, you know where my office is located.

Monologue #25 Lawyer

Hello. A courtroom may seem like a strange place to conduct an interview, but I invited you here for an important reason.

To be clear, the subject of this interview is the transferable skills of theatre to my profession as an attorney, is that correct? Good.

Yes, I studied theatre extensively both in high school and college. I knew I wanted to be a trial lawyer from an early age, and theatre is a great way to prepare for trial work.

That brings me back to the reason I wanted to meet you in a courtroom. I'm about to make a bold statement. A courtroom is a theatre. I don't mean that it is like a theatre. I mean that there is no specific reason for public trials to be conducted the way we conduct them. It could all be handled in writing and through other means of communication, but there is something about this ancient method of gathering and hearing witnesses and bringing forth evidence that speaks to the quest for justice. Those other forms of communication are dry. They are lacking in the human element so we hold court, and a courtroom is literally a theatre.

As an attorney, I am a playwright. I have a story to tell, and everything and everyone I present to the court will play some part in telling that story. When I call a witness to the stand, my purpose is not merely to get them to speak truth. My purpose is to show the court their character. The opposing attorney is a collaborator on the script, but the opposing attorney will try to pull the story in a different direction.

The judge is the director in this theatre.

I learned a lot about wardrobe in my theatre studies, and I know that when I walk into a courtroom it's important for me to look the part of a highly trained, experienced, attorney at law. I'll let you in on a secret. I have dressed like certain TV lawyers on certain occasions, and I'm not the only lawyer that has. Associations matter. It's all about looking like you belong in your role. So I wear business suits, always cleaned and pressed. I carry a briefcase.

Acting is a big part of what I do. I mean expressing things a certain way. At this time I am a prosecuting attorney. It is important for me to treat the accused with a certain amount of disdain. The defense attorney will treat the accused with a certain amount of warmth and closeness.

If I put a victim on the stand or a witness who is sympathetic to the victim, it is important that they act out their pain. The jury, which is the ultimate audience, needs to understand the hurt the accused has caused. This can be tricky. If a witness comes across as phony, it backfires.

Finally I will say that being a part of a theatre audience is a skill itself. Some people pick up on so much more than others. As an attorney, I have to be able to pick up on many things as witnesses give testimony. If I hear a crack in a witness' voice, is that because they are thirsty or because they lied about something? Do the stories I am hearing contradict or can they be reconciled?

You're welcome. I enjoyed meeting you too.

Monologue #26 Marine Biologist

Welcome to the sea lab. Out the window on the ocean side we may get to see the sunset during the interview. It's almost time.

I'm going to tell you about how I learned skills in theatre that transfer to my career in marine biology. I got involved with theatre mainly in college. I was drawn in by the social side of it. I only took a couple of classes, but I got heavily involved with the production and promotion of plays on campus. It was fun and meaningful, and yes, I learned some transferable skills.

I say that with a "yes" to emphasize that you would not expect a science job to use a lot of art. What I mean is, when people think of marine biology, they seem to associate what we do with swimming with dolphins and riding on boats. Some marine biologists never do much of either. It is largely about the studying of the chemical/biological content of water at the microbial level. As for going out and making direct observations of marine life, I have been fortunate to have had a couple of opportunities to do offshore surveys, and that's the first area where my involvement in theatre has come in handy.

Like I said, I was always more into the production and promotion side of theatre. Those ocean surveys last for weeks at a time. I realized we would get bored and maybe a little lonely out on the deep seas so I took along some board games, some movies that I dare say are of high quality, and some small decorations for throwing birthday parties. I held and promoted a couple of event nights each week. I would start talking about it a couple of days in advance, maybe even do an announcement over the ship PA system. I tried to give it a feel of excitement, and I believe it really did bring some joy to our down time at sea.

But for a more direct use of my skill: Marine biology depends on government agencies, government grants, and grants from foundations. Funding is a constant concern, and in order to get funds, I often have to help with grant writing. Grant writing is how an organization with a mission communicates what they do and what its needs are to an organization that provides money. Fortunately we have a professional grant writer, but it is up to me to tell the grant writer the ongoing story of our work. My involvement in theatre taught me a lot about the methods of storytelling. I have to give the grant writer the vision and words to convey the importance and urgency of what we do.

Finally there are those extremely rare opportunities to just go out in a boat and maybe even take a swim with the dolphins. Those moments are important for public relations and to show a human side to what we do. It's important to take pictures, and I learned a lot about photography in theatre, especially in connection with preparing promotional flyers.

Oh look, the sun is almost done setting. I've enjoyed the interview. You're welcome. Please tell your teacher I said hi.

Monologue #27 Detective

Thanks for meeting me here at this diner and coffee shop. Police officers frequent this place regularly. Soda of your choice on me.

Your teacher tells me you are here to interview me about how the skills I learned in theatre translate into my work as a detective. That's kinda funny. I'm always the one interviewing suspects and others with information so this should be fun. I work for the city police department

In college I studied forensic science, which is what a detective uses in the investigation of crimes. I double majored in criminal justice, but I took all my electives in the area of theatre. Before that, I took theatre in highschool.

The first skill that I can think of that transfers from theatre to detective work is writing. Remember not all plays are fictional. Some are about actual events. Those events have to be interpreted and laid out in a coherent fashion. That skill is foundational to forensic science.

Let's say that I am called to a home where a car has been stolen. I ask many questions. When was the car last driven? When was it last seen? Did anyone else have a key? Then I ask neighbors what they saw? I try to locate security cameras in the area that may offer any information. Once I have all the information I can gather, I construct a timeline of the events. In order to do that I have to visualize the events. That is just like writing a play. Finally, if we charge a suspect, I present the play in court by calling witnesses to tell the story and confirm the timeline.

Now let me tell you a secret. The vast majority of crimes have an inside element. Sometimes the person that reports the crime did the crime. Even where there is not an inside element, people have secrets, and people lie. A big part of my job is discerning truth and lies. One of the skills I rely on to do that, I developed it in theatre classes by playing games like. I watch for people's micro expressions, the little tell tale signs on their face about how they really feel about what they are telling me.

One more really big skill that I use is simply acting. When I interview a suspect the first time, I usually tell them that they are not a suspect and that we just need some information from them to help pin the crime on another person. That's right. It's a lie. I then act extremely nonchalantly while I'm interviewing them, like I don't suspect anything. Sometimes the more convinced I act of their story, the more they talk. I'm so nice to them sometimes they just go and go until finally their story is full of contradictions. The second time I tell them I need clarification on some points of the story, but I take a uniformed officer or two with me to arrest them if they begin to suspect I'm onto them.

Hey, you're welcome, and I have to tell you this interview has brought back some good memories. Glad to have done it. Thank your teacher for me.

Monologue #28 Exercise Trainer

Come on in this gym! Yeah! Not only am I going to tell you the skills I learned in theatre that I use in my gym, I'm going to show you!

You look like you could use a work out. Firstly, there's acting! If I'm not excited about working out, how can I expect my clients to be? So I have to feel it, and I have to make sure they feel it.

Come on, let's do some jumping jacks! Yeah, Whoo! Boom boom yeah, that's some great music! Now you're breathing. Glad you wore those tennis shoes!

Ha ha! Now let's kick it into overdrive. Five more, four more, three more, two more, and STOP! Okay, you can rest now. I'll show you some other stuff.

Each one of my clients gets a personal work out. The goal is to start them out slowly and then get them up to their maximum potential. Here ya go, take a look at the form I use. It includes places to keep up with each exercise they do and then to write down goals. The goals that I write down in one session becomes the script for the next session. It helps the client visualize their growth and success.

When a client is working out, well, in a sense I have my director's hat on. Speaking of which, why don't you pick up those small hand weights right there. Now lift them over your head. Yeah! Feel that muscle burn! You're getting stronger! Come on another rep, I believe you can do it. You've got that look in your eye. Nothing can stop you!

See I just directed you as you did a set of overhead lifts.

Being the owner of a small business these days usually requires online promotion. When I opened my gym, I made a video and put it on the internet showing this place off and telling the whole world what I offered here. That's two theatre skills right there! I used things I learned on the production and promotion side of theatre.

Ok, one more exercise now. Pull yourself up on this bar and do some chin ups. My assistant will stand by to make sure you don't fall. I'm going to turn the music up. Now let's rock some chin ups! Yeah! I'll do some over here on this bar.

And that's an important skill for an exercise trainer-- the ability to sympathize. I feel the burn that you're feeling, but let's keep going. And three more, two more, one more… and… one to grow on!! Oh yeah!!!

The last thing I'll mention is my involvement with set building. People respond to the patterns they recognize. So it is important that this gym looks and feels like a gym. Some of these pieces of equipment are seldom used. I'm not even sure how to use a couple of the extensions, but it's important to have them here for the atmosphere. It is conducive to working out.

Hey! I had a blast! Hope you did too! Tell your teacher it was a blast!

Monologue #29 Financial Consultant

Hi, welcome to the firm. We'll sit here in the lobby if that's okay with you. Nothing but computers and file cabinets in the back. I'll have our receptionist bring up a round of bottled waters.

As I understand your teacher's request, I am to tell you about how studying theatre when I was young helped develop some skills that I now use as a Financial Consultant.

First I should tell you what I do. I help people plan for the economic aspect of their life. My clients include young people who are just starting their careers. They often are looking for a way to use their earnings to balance their lives. Some of my clients are people who have just come into large amounts of money. This includes lottery winners, the beneficiaries of wills, and people who win lawsuits. They want to know how to manage their money to make the most use of it and to make it last as long as possible. Middle aged people come to me to help them begin planning for retirement. Sometimes retirees come to me to help figure out how to live on their retirement earnings, especially if their earnings are small. Even in difficult cases, we can at least help with good budgeting skills and inform them of various kinds of financial assistance and services that are available to them.

The first theatre skill that comes to mind is character analysis. When I meet a new client, we start with a picture of where they are and what their current financial situation is. Let's say that a couple comes to me right after their children are grown and out of the house and we conclude that the house they are living in is now too large and costs too much in upkeep. Maybe they would rather not sell the house for sentimental reasons, but upkeep on the average house costs 5% of the total value of the house per year. The couple could plan to do all the physical work themselves, and that's where I come in? I have to ask them if they are prepared to climb up on a roof, rip old roofing off, and nail on new shingles? Are they really that committed? Are they really going to crawl around under the house when a pipe breaks and do the work of a plumber? A few might, but most will not. My job is to help my clients know themselves and to be realistic with their plans.

Another skill is script writing. In a sense, a budget is a script for the use of money and resources. After we go through a thorough analysis of where and who the client is, we start to plan for the future. If the client has just come into money this typically means investing for the long terms in stable markets or even putting money into something more certain such as an annuity. An annuity pays you out in small increments sometimes for the rest of your life. If a person knows they have trouble with over spending this can be a helpful option.

Thank you for coming by. I hope this has helped.

Monologue #30 Counselor/Psychologist

Hello. I hope you don't mind meeting out of doors like this, but I didn't think it would be appropriate to meet at the office complex. Our patients value their anonymity, you understand. Plus this is a nice place to get some fresh air and sunshine.

Your theatre teacher, who is an old friend of mine, asked me to give you an interview about theatre skills that I use in my professional life as a psychological counselor. I am honored that she thought of me. Ordinarily I am the one doing most of the listening and taking notes. This gives me a better sense of how my clients may feel.

I was involved with plays from a very early age and took theatre in high school and college. I met your teacher at college. I felt that taking theatre would give me extra insight into the human psyche, but we'll come back to that.

The first skill that theatre helped me with was the ability to pay attention to and appreciate a story. Theatre involvement isn't all about performing, you know. It's as much about absorbing the plays and the literature behind them. When you're watching a play, you owe it to yourself to get completely caught up in it.

As a counselor, I have to be an active, avid listener. Sometimes my clients have many years of secrets that they need to unload. Sometimes they have been through trauma, and they need catharsis. That simply means getting the thoughts and feelings they have out and being heard. They need to know they are not alone and that someone understands. Certainly getting into plays helped with my ability to listen and to really sympathize.

Although I never did any work as a director, I got to see many directors in action, and I picked up a thing or two from the good ones. Part of my job is leading support groups. For example, I lead grief support groups for people who have just lost a loved one. The participants gather in a circle and they take turns sharing their struggles and their pain. There is an element of theatre in this practice, and I serve as the director. They aren't allowed to talk over one another. There is a loose agenda for each session. Between sessions there is journaling and reading. This creates a sense of motion so that everyone doesn't come together and repeat the same things every week. I gently push each participant to work through their pain. It is good therapy. Maybe theatre itself offers some therapeutic value.

Finally, I will say that I have to be fully aware that when I am seeing a client, I am playing a role. I'm not just a buddy or a pal. I am a Doctor of Psychology. My clients come to me for help with managing serious problems. I have to remain focused on that. I have to understand the part I am playing. I am never fake with my clients. Being fake would damage the process, but I really do have to be focused on the role they see me playing.

You're welcome. It's been a pleasure meeting you too.

Monologue #31 Painter

Hi, welcome to my art studio. It's a converted sunroom, the main reason I bought this house. The view is wide open and it gets maximum lighting.

If I understand correctly I am supposed to explain how I learned skills in theatre that I used in my career as a painter.

In my experience, when most people think of a professional, artistic painter, they think of some famous artist from the past whose work is collectible and they think that painting is an easy way to get rich. For over 99% of us painters, this is not true at all. It is hard work that requires a lot of discipline, and we are fortunate if it provides our sole income. My highest degree is called a Master of Fine Arts. In some fields it would be the equivalent of a doctorate.

Another thing that people seem to believe is that artists work entirely off of inspiration and impulse, but the fact is, most of the work that we do is commission. Someone may hire me to do a portrait of their family. Now, I certainly try to find inspiration and bring style to everything I do, but I need to be clear about what it is I do. I've painted magazine covers, murals in shopping centers, commemorations of special events, portraits of everything from children to pets to the houses people live in. I do a certain amount of painting with the intention of selling, and those usually follow a theme. For example, I've done several hundred beach scenes, and I sell those at arts and crafts festivals in coastal areas. I also run an online store. I also teach classes at the local community college and offer lessons here in my studio. I stay busy. What I do has taken me places I never would have gone otherwise, but it really is hard work.

I've always had a knack for art so I gravitated to the set building and decorating side. Let's say there was a play set in the old west. I would paint a window, as if the characters were inside looking out, complete with tumble weeds and cacti. Or maybe the story was set on a ship. I would paint an ocean backdrop. So painting, my life's work, is one skill that I got to practice in theatre.

But indirectly, what I've learned is that succeeding as an artist is all about presentation and reputation. Let's say that I'm selling my work from a tent in a small town art festival. Everything from the quality of the tent to the clothes I wear to the way I conduct myself with the customers has an impact on how much I sell. I have to look the part of an artist.

The art itself has to be displayed to fully show its beauty and really catch the eye. All of these skills are part of theatre. I learned a lot from watching directors blocking. The technical side of theatre, especially the use of light comes into my presentations of art.

I hope this has been helpful. I see that one of my students is arriving. Have a nice afternoon.

Monologue #32 Reporter

Come on in. Glad to have you. As you can tell this office complex greatly exceeds our needs. At our peak, you would have heard ten typewriters going at any given moment. Print journalism isn't what it used to be. We now print twice weekly, but this newspaper used to print twice daily. Of course we have a continual electronic presence now, and we have partnered with a local radio station to provide news since they can no longer afford a full time news staff.

I've conducted hundreds if not thousands of interviews over the years, but I believe this is the first time I've been answering the questions, and I believe the main question is how did theatre provide me wil skills that I use in my career as a reporter?

I grew up in a small town and my family was involved in community theatre. My parents insisted that I take theatre classes all the way through school. They loved theatre and wanted me to share their joy, and I did.

The first and most obvious skill that I had opportunities to develop in theatre classes is writing. Playwriting assignments taught me the power of visualization. I had to find a way to make the audience see what I saw to hear what I heard. That's what good reporting is.

A reporter is a stand in for the reader. I ask questions about the things the reader would naturally want to know. In that sense, I am an actor. I play the voice of John Q. Public.

Consider what happens at a press conference. The physical act of a press conference is not really necessary and hasn't been for at least a hundred and fifty years and maybe longer. Reporters could telegraph their questions to public figures, and the public figures could send well thought out answers, but there is a certain energy that a press conference generates. The public figures who give them make themselves vulnerable to press interrogation. The public figures play their part. We reporters play ours. It is theatre.

To be a good reporter, I have to be bold. I can't be shy. The most important questions I ask will not be soft or easy to answer. In some circumstances it is important to catch someone off guard, as rude as that may sound, but prepared answers are often less than honest. I learned a lot about boldness through theatre involvement.

The last thing I would mention is that being involved with different aspects of theatre taught me to work under deadlines and to time everything accordingly. As a reporter I am constantly under deadlines. Even with the online edition, it's important to report stories while they are at peak relevance. The production of a play happens on a schedule, from the selection of the play to the casting to the practice schedule there is timing. The presentation of a play is a timed event from start to finish. Every person involved with a play in every aspect of it has to be aware of time. Time skill certainly translates into what I do as a reporter.

You're welcome. I've enjoyed being on the other side of an interview.

Monologue #33 Sandwich Chef

Welcome to the deli. Why don't you sit here at the sandwich bar? Not only will I tell you about the skills I learned in theatre that transfer to my work, I will show you some of them.

I did not get into theatre until college, but when I got into it, I really got into it. I enjoyed the people who were into theatre. I've always had a lot of energy, and theatre was a great place for me to use it. I took classes all four years of college, and I participated in plays mostly as an actor, but I was always apt to help out on the technical side when a hand was needed.

I realized in college that I wanted to do something entrepreneurial, and this deli is the result. I had worked in the restaurant business going back to high school. I am a highly social person. I love to hear people's stories. I love to participate in the lives of many people so it just made sense that I would open a business such as this one.

Have you ever gone into a sandwich shop only to be greeted by a dead face behind the counter? Have you ever seen a sandwich stuck together like the maker just wanted to get done with making it and get on to the next customer? Well, that is not the kind of service you will get here. I insist that each chef make each sandwich with attention to detail, energy, and flair. I learned a lot about these things in theatre, and theatre definitely provided me with these intangible skills that transfer directly into my work.

All businesses are built on relationships. I know many of my customers by name. It's important that I know what they generally like and that I recognize their moods as they come into the deli. Different theatre games that we played in college helped develop this type of skill.

In ways, this deli is a lot like a theatre. The moment the customer walks in, they are greeted vocally. We try to convey a feeling that this is a friendly place. We want them to walk out feeling better than when they came in. The sandwich making process is part of that. I teach all my chefs to work with physical charisma. I learned a lot about that in theatre studies. We lay the bread out first, then add each layer as we make conversation with each customer about their taste. Making the sandwich is a collaboration and a show. We want each customer to feel that they are getting something special.

Finally I would mention that a lot of work in a deli is clean up. It is mopping at the end of the day. It is hauling out scraps and paper waste. It is washing and folding. Something I learned in theatre, which includes taking down sets and cleaning up physical facilities, is to make this kind of work as fast and as enjoyable as possible. I try to find music that everyone can agree on, and hopefully the process goes like a well rehearsed dance number.

You're welcome. The sandwich is on the house.

Monologue #34 Mayor

Hello and welcome to city hall. Since this is a small town, all of our administrative offices are in this one complex. Police chief is right over there. Utilities are over on the other side. Court is down the hall.

Your teacher has asked me to tell you how my involvement with theatre sharpened skills that I use as a mayor.

I was always an extroverted person and heavily involved with school and community activities. I was one of those persons who would go to school then stay out for play rehearsals or sports involvement or anything else I could find to do every night I could. I don't mean to brag, but I always was a go getter.

The first area where theatre furnished me with some important skills is campaigning. I walked the streets of this town. I shook many hands. I sat in the coffee shops and listened to what the locals had to say, and I took notes on a big yellow pad. I went out and got to know the town and let the town get to know me. If that's not theatrical, I don't know what is. There is some acting involved with campaigning. A campaign requires production skills too. You have to know when to do what, when to say what. I often said things that sounded off the cuff but were in fact scripted.

An obvious area where I use theatre skills is in the ceremonial life of the town. Let's say that a new judge takes office, It is my role to swear them into office. Same goes for police chiefs, who in turn swears in each officer. Every year the city parks department puts up holiday lights, and when we turn them on, it is my job to give a brief speech. Same goes for new years day and Independence day. If someone famous comes to town I might give them the key to the city to mark the occasion. Let's say that a car parts manufacturer is considering locating a small factory here to make brake pads and let's say that i get word that one of their executives is coming to town. I would give them the key to the city. It would be a gesture that means we receive them with honor and respect. Hopefully it would help persuade them to locate here. All of these ceremonial acts are strongly theatrical. They each make a statement. They each have an underlying script, and it's usually written down.

Another part of my job is the regular public meetings with the city council. That's where we answer questions from the public. That is where various ordinances are debated and passed… or not passed. There is reality to what we do of course, but there is a theatrical element to it. Let's say that the council member from district three holds a position that is not held by the rest of the council. Let's say the position is popular only in their district. That council member may argue knowing there is no chance it will affect the outcome of a vote. They do it for show for their constituents. That's how politics works. So always be on the lookout for it.

You're welcome. Have a nice afternoon.

Monologue #35 TV Weather Reporter

Hi, welcome to the studio. This is where we produce local television news programming. We schedule four broadcasts most days of the week: morning, noon, evening, and night, and sometimes we air short segments for important breaking news or emergency broadcasts. We also upload segments to our internet site so that the public can view at their leisure.

Meteorology, which is the study of the weather, was my major in college, but I took every course I could that involved public speaking including many theatre courses. I realized I would need the skills to do this job.

The first skill I would mention is the ability to read a script and really understand where my character fits in it. The station is constantly receiving weather updates from the national weather service. My job as a professional meteorologist is to be able to interpret the reports and apply them locally.

After I interpret the weather reports, I have to quickly write a script for myself, which is what I will say on the air. I usually do this in the form of an outline. Unless there is a major weather event, I simply report the basics in a pretty standard format: temperature forecasts, precipitation forecasts, cloud coverage, that sort of thing.

My weather segment script then fits into the broader script of the news broadcasts. I take my cues from the producer/director. It involves a lot of timing because we do our broadcasts live. There is no editing. I don't get a second take.

Of course since I do the weather live, that means that I have to look professional. We have someone in the studio who helps with make up, but I am responsible for my own wardrobe. As you can see I dress in business attire.

Possibly the most important skill I learned from studying theatre is acting. Most of the time, I speak in a calm manner, but during catastrophic weather, I become the voice of safety. Thunderstorms, hurricanes, tornadoes, and floods, all of these pose a threat to human life. It is my job to convince people to make decisions on the side of safety during times of severe weather. They have to be able to feel the concern in my voice and mannerisms.

I'm sure you remember the tornadoes that struck on a tuesday evening about three months ago. I was in the studio at the time the weather moved into the viewing area. We stopped other programming, and I got on the air and began to plead with people to take shelter in their basements or storm shelters, and if they didn't have them to get into their bathtubs or in hallways. My voice also went out over our sister radio station's broadcast. I told drivers to get under cement bridges if possible.

I spoke with as much urgency as I could. Acting is largely about just tapping into the real emotions that we all have rather than faking. That's what I did that day.

I have had several people contact me since then to thank me for the report. They took action, and it protected them from the storms.

You're welcome, and thank you. The weather will be fine for you to walk home.

Monologue #36 Museum Curator

Hi, welcome to the regional history museum. You've come at an interesting time. We're doing an exhibit of photographs capturing street life for as long as the streets in this area have been photographed, which is at least the past one hundred and sixty years, plus there's a whole lot more to see.

We can talk as we stroll. I believe I am supposed to tell you about the skills I gained in theatre that transfer into my work.

My undergraduate degree is in history, but I took theatre all through college. Theatre is a major transmitter of history. Some plays are written with history in mind, but at some point, every play becomes historical. The plays written during the 1950's for example, teach us a lot about the history of that time period. We gain insight into the technologies and culture of whatever time a play is set. Even plays set in the distant future reflect back on the concerns of the time in which they were written.

See this photo here from the time of the war? I acted in a play that was set in the war, and of course our costumes looked like what you see in this photo. I recognized the general time period in part because of my background in theatre. Knowledge is interconnected like that, and the more you learn, the more you can learn.

See the uniform in the display case at the end of the hall? It's also from the war. I worked on getting ready for public viewing using skills I practiced doing wardrobe work in theatre.

Speaking of the war, a war is an example of a story that a museum tells. Some museums are dedicated entirely to one war. The practice I gained in theatre classes, learning to think as a visual storyteller, is an important skill to use in a museum. A museum exhibit is a lot like a play.

Another use of playwriting skills is in developing tours. We have staff here who will take you on a tour of the museum and point out fun and interesting facts. It helps maximize the museum experience and provides depth of understanding. They don't do that off the top of their heads. The tours are written, and as curator, I am the main writer. The tour guides, you've already noticed, dress in costumes from different periods of the region's history. There goes someone from the 1700's. And as I've already mentioned theatre provides experience in costuming.

We get many exhibits in and out, but some of our displays never change. For example, the hand made canoe near the entrance has always been here and likely always will because it is an artifact of the first people to inhabit the area. The last item on display at this time is a copy of the most recent newspaper. There is a placard beside it pointing out that the canoe and the physical paper on which the news is printed come from the same kind of tree that grows native in this area. It is all one story, and in a sense a museum is a theater of time.

Thank you for coming out. I have to go to my office, but you're welcome to look around more.

Monologue #37 Copywriter

Hi. Thank you for meeting me here at the shopping center. I felt this would be the perfect place for someone to conduct an interview with a copywriter. After all, as a copywriter, it is my job to write words that sell stuff. In a nutshell, that's what I do.

If I understand correctly, this will be an interview about skills I learned or strengthened in theatre and how they transfer into my work. My involvement in theatre goes all the way back to childhood. I was in plays both in school and in civic organizations. I took classes most of the years I was in school.

My work is to write about things in such a way that people want to buy them. For example, I might get a contract with the producer of a website that sells shoes. I would write a description of the shoes and what makes them desirable. I would talk about how comfortable the shoes are, how stylish they are, how durable.

Suppose one kind is a work shoe, I would write something like "Feel light on your feet all day long! These shoes are designed to be light as air and to provide maximum comfort. They come in four colors: black, white, brown, and blue. The upper part of the shoe is made of leather for comfort but coated with plastic to resist water. The sole of the shoe is durable, no-slip rubber. Small perforations on the side ensure maximum breathability so as to keep your feet cool and dry. Designed with input from those who wear them, this is one of the best engineered shoes of the decade!"

I learned a lot about reading and writing in theatre. Some of the earliest reading I ever did was my scripts. I was eager to learn my lines as a child. As I got older, the reading became more advanced, and I was given writing assignments. A good play has words that just pop off the page, words that really hold your interest, and that's the sort of writing I have to do in my job as a copywriter.

At the college level, I held a position in the theatre club. You guessed it, director of promotions. One of my jobs was to make flyers to promote productions of plays and the theatre club itself. I would get a small team together and we would assemble things like pictures of the actors in costume, colored paper, and glitter. We would promote the play as an evening of entertainment and fun. I would also advertise in the school newspaper, which came out every other week. I would talk theatre up in the school cafeteria and other hang out spots on campus. I would go to sporting events and hand out the flyers. And it all worked. We always had good attendance when I was in that position.

I would tell anyone going into copywriting to get involved with theatre. It's a great training ground. My involvement in theatre was ultimately like those work shoes I was telling you about. I learned things that are simple, practical, and foundational.

Glad I could help you out. Good luck.

Monologue #38 Park Ranger

Hi, welcome to the park. Glad to have you here at the station. We are on the side of a mountain here, and you can look out and see the expanse all the way to the river.

I understand that I will be telling you about the skills I learned in theatre that transfer into my job as a park ranger.

I took theatre in highschool for two years and then for three semesters in college. I did a little acting, but I worked mainly on the technical side of things.

I don't think most people realize that a park ranger is a law enforcement officer, or maybe they only half realize it. Only on the rarest of occasions would I use my authority as a law enforcement officer outside of the park, but I took law enforcement training, I have been deputized, and I have the ability to do things like write citations and even make arrests.

Fortunately I seldom have to do enforcement of regular laws. The vast majority of what I enforce is park rules. When you use the park, the rules are part of a contract. You agree to keep these rules just by being here.

As a law enforcement officer, I wear a costume, my uniform. It has badges to convey my authority. It is made of cloth dyed forest and earth colors to indicate my connection to the land and the park itself. Most people recognize a ranger when they see one, and that's the point. That is theatre, especially costuming.

Let's say I discover litter at a campsite. I have to take command of the situation. I am not a very loud person by nature, but I did work on projecting myself when I studied theatre. It helps. So I would start by giving a firm yet respectful command to clean the campsite. I would explain that wildlife comes into these areas and that it poses a risk both to the wildlife and campers. Usually that is enough, but if I am ignored, I write a ticket.

Only a few times have I ever had to arrest someone and that was when intoxication was involved… on their part. Even if I am arresting someone who is intoxicated, there is a script I have to follow.

On the positive side of ranger work, it is my job to instill a love of the land, to really show off the beauty of what we have preserved. On the technical side of theatre I learned a lot about lighting and building props and sets. You learn to keep in mind the point of view of the person who has never seen the play before, and as we design walking trails, look out points, trail markers, and signs, we must do the same. I must always work from the point of view of the first time visitor to the park.

I never actually directed a play, but I watched and I learned from directors, especially the way they completely immersed their minds in the play. Twice I have directed search and rescue operations in the park. Both times were successful. Both times I immersed myself in events as they unfolded.

I hope you enjoyed your afternoon. Thanks for coming out.

Monologue #39 Convenience Store Manager

Hello, come on in. You must be the student here for the interview. Why don't you help yourself to a soda from the soda fountain, and while you're at it get me one too, strawberry.

Now I believe you're here to find out how I learned some skills in my drama classes that come into play in my work as a convenience store manager? Is that about the gist of it?

Okay, good. I've been thinking it over since your teacher asked me to do this, and I believe I can give you some examples. I never went to college, but I took theatre in most of my school years. I was always pretty good at it, usually got a speaking part in plays.

Convenience stores are all about high volume sales and that means everyone who works in one has to do their job fast. We have to get the customer in and out of the door fast. We have to be a team with timing, and that's a lot like the cast and crew of a play. Time is always of the essence in this line of work. Time is always of the essence in theatre. The ability to work in a group with a high amount of timing, that's a skill that I definitely use every day. It can be stressful, but it can be fun. It makes the time go by faster. Rarely is there a dull moment around here.

One of my favorite things in my theatre studies was improv. We usually ended up having a good laugh. In a business like this, I am faced with situations every day where I have to think on my feet. A sales rep could come in and try to get me to carry a new kind of candy bar. I have to be able to evaluate the situation fast. I have to be able to read the sales rep. Or maybe a customer will come back and say that a banana they just bought had a soft spot and they want their money back. Can I trust them? It's always something like this, ya know. You have to think fast. I definitely use improv skills.

My high school drama teacher insisted that we do all the work so I helped a lot with getting props ready and blocking. I had a pretty good knack for knowing what went where. I developed it deeper in theatre and use it here in the convenience store. Sometimes I will put up a shelf of beef jerky or potato chips, then walk outside, then walk back inside so I can tell how it's going to catch the eye of the customer. Everything has to be eye-catching. And there's a logical order to where everything goes.

Working in the convenience store business, I am constantly having to memorize things. A customer rushes in, their car is low on oil, and they just need one container of it. I quickly tell them, "aisle four, shelf two, just below the brake fluid." We don't have much of any one thing, but we have a little of many things. And I have to know my customers too. So many of them are regulars. Memorization is a skill theatre really develops that I use here all the time.

You're welcome. Have a great day.

Monologue #40 Math Teacher

The cafeteria seems like the best place to do this interview since we have lunch at the same time. Your theatre teacher and I used to take theatre courses together, and I am delighted that I got picked for this interview.

As I understand, the subject of this interview is the transferable skills of theatre. You may be surprised that as a math teacher, I use theatre skills every day. We'll come back to that. I have a master's degree in math education, and what that means is that I have had many teachers and professors. I added it up one time, and I've had well over a hundred instructors. Math is a hard subject to make exciting, but some made it interesting, and I think that's a fair goal.

Math does not have to be a dull subject. Math can involve creativity, high levels of visualization, and big surprises. I know some folks in the math field like to keep things abstract, but I love to see the real life uses of math, and there are many. Nearly everything we do in human life involves math. I realize not every class can be wildly entertaining, but it is my job to make each class as interesting as possible.

In theatre I got involved in the making of props, and something that I find helps my classes is props to help them visualize the practical use of math. Let's say that in geometry we are doing the lessons on finding the volume of a cone. I will bring a big plastic ice cream cone. We will measure it, and then my students get busy calculating how much ice cream it would take to fill it if it were real.

A significant percentage of my students will work in housing at some point in their life. I have a model house that I keep in the back of the class so that whenever a math principle relates to a house, I bring it up front. How many bricks are in a wall? How many square feet in a two story house? How many shingles on the roof? You get the idea. I'm a big believer in props.

I am not a talkative person by nature it would seem. I wouldn't call myself shy, just quiet. Theatre helped me learn to open up more, to project more. I always enjoyed the energy of my theatre classes. We used so many parts of our brains, not just the analytical parts.

Theatre helped develop my creativity, and I enjoy the creativity involved with planning lessons. One of my favorite activities is to take students outside and have them use trigonometry to measure various things like the number of square yards on the football field or the height of the flagpole. It has some of the qualities of a show. Each student comes back with a different story to tell. Did you know that even music has a mathematical basis? Music and theatre have gone hand in hand since before recorded time.

You're welcome. I enjoyed sharing my thoughts with you. Next year, if you sign up for one of my math classes, I'll try to make it interesting.

Monologue #41 Dry Cleaner/Clothing Repairer

Hello. I will meet you on the bench out front. Let me grab a couple of bottled waters.

Pleasure to meet you. So I'm giving you an interview about some skills I honed in theatre that transfer to my job as the owner/operator of a general purpose clothes cleaning and restoring business. We do it all here, you see, dry cleaning, full service cleaning, sewing, you name it, if your clothes need it, we do it.

I am the third generation of my family to go into this line of work. Some of the skills I have, I developed in childhood, but my involvement with local theatre and school theatre helped develop the skills.

Obviously I got involved with the wardrobe and costuming side of things. That is how my family first made contact with the theatre world. Local theatre companies and schools brought interesting work for my grandparents so they got the next generation involved. Then my generation got involved.

Let's take buttons. An older costume loses a button or two ever so often. Well, I've been collecting buttons since childhood. I know what kind of buttons they wore at what times in history. I've got buttons from many decades. I've got metal buttons, wooden buttons, stone buttons, and plastic buttons. I've got upper class buttons and lower class buttons. I've got business buttons and military buttons. Theatre gave me plenty of opportunities to develop myself as the local buttons expert, which in this line of work in this town I'm known for.

Every piece of clothing we wear is part of a costume. We are always communicating things with our wardrobe. Even the ancient Spartans, as rough and tough as they tried to be, wore matching uniforms. Even in battle, they wanted to look good and to match.

No matter what kind of clothing I am cleaning or repairing, I am keenly aware of how it will be used as a costume. If I am working on a dress for a wedding, I am aware and envisioning the person wearing it. I picture the wedding. If I am working on a mechanic's uniform, I imagine the mechanic looking professional. I mean, who wants to take their car to a ragged mechanic? Everyone wants to look the part they are playing in life. I do costume maintenance for everyone.

Being more involved with wardrobe and making things, I learned about dyes and the effects of colors in theatre. It's a skill I use doing cloth repair and stain removal. I have to be able to blend colors evenly and gradually. Sometimes it's impossible to restore something perfectly, but I can usually get pretty close.

I guess the last thing I'll mention is that running a shop involves a lot of theatricality, no matter what kind of shop it is. Customers have to feel comfortable, and creating that feeling involves presentation. It would be easy enough to bring my completed work out in a basket and say "here," but I wrap fresh clothes in paper or plastic. I attach labels that play up the details of everything we did.

Thank you for your interest. Here's some coupons you can take home. Take care.

Monologue #42 Hardware Store Manager

Hey, come on in. You must be the student who's interviewing me about the skills I learned in theatre and how they relate to my work as a Hardware Store Manager.

I've never been interviewed before, and I never gave the subject much thought, but I'm looking forward to it. I was hired into this store right after high school. I worked as a clerk for a few years, then shift manager, and then two years ago, they made me general manager of the store.

When the folks in this town talk about me, they usually say I'm a "character."

"The manager down there at the hardware store is quite a character," they say.

Is it not interesting that they pick a term from the world of theatre to label me? I take it as a compliment. It means that I'm interesting.

Some theatre skills that I use in hardware will be obvious. For example, I have to know where every item we sell is located in the store. It helps tremendously if I know how the item is used and can give customers advice. Everything we sell is available cheaper online. Our customers come to us for two reasons. One is immediate availability. If someone's washing machine needs to be installed, rather than save a dollar on the connection hose and wait three days, they will usually just come here and get it straight off the shelf.

Sometimes the customer knows more or less what to do. They just need to hammer down a few of the details That's where my memory for the uses of each item comes into play.

That brings me to another theatre skill, which I had the opportunity to practice in script writing assignments. When I am helping a customer I have to be able to see their needs. I have to put myself in their shows, so to speak, the way a script writer has to know the mind of each character in a play.

Once I have a clear understanding of what the customer needs, I go into director mode giving them a script so to speak for how to fix the problem. Let's say someone's attic exhaust fan needs to be replaced. I will sell them the fan, the physical connection bolts, the electrical connections, and the sealant. I always worry about customer safety so I give them directions in that area.

I used to help build sets and some skills I picked up in that process come into use in a hardware store. Presentation makes a big difference. It's important for instance that our main products are at eye level for customer perusal. The products that we stock need to jump off the shelves visually. For example, many tools are chrome plated. It's not necessary that they be, but there is nothing like chrome to make a tool catch the eye of a customer. In terms of visual presentation, this hardware store has a lot in common with a stage.

You're welcome. I appreciate your interest. Have a nice afternoon.

Monologue #43 Diplomat

Greetings. There's a breakroom down the hall where we can talk. As I understand, I am supposed to give you an interview about the skills I learned in theatre and how they are involved in what I do as an officer of the Foreign Service, or as most people would call me, a Diplomat.

Let's say you have two countries. One country is located on an island, and the people of that country make their living mostly by fishing. The other country is located on a continent, and the people of that country make their living mostly by making things. It would benefit the people of the island country to be able to sell fish to the people who live in the other country. It would benefit the people who live in the country where they make things to be able to sell what they make to the people who live in the island country, especially fishing boats.

What these two countries could use is a trade relationship, and as a Diplomat I would be involved with working out the rules for how they trade. When goods are shipped into a country tariffs are usually paid. If a food item is coming into a country it has to be inspected to make sure that it is healthy to be eaten. When the people who work on the ships come into a port, they need permission to be able to go ashore and travel.

There are many small details to be worked out in the relationships between nations. And then these details have to be enforced. The politicians can't do it, and that's where diplomats come in. Let's say that you were in a foreign country and lost your passport, which is the document that allows you to be there in the first place. You have no way to prove who you are and no way to get back home. You would seek the help of diplomats from your country that work in the foreign country. They would work with diplomats from the foreign country and hopefully resolve the situation quickly so you can go back home.

I studied theatre in high school and college. The most important things I learned that apply to my work came from the content of the plays. The best playwrights, the ones whose names are known to the world, have a wonderful understanding of human motivations. If I am involved with negotiations on behalf of my country, I need to understand what is driving the diplomats from the other country. I also need to understand the individuals I am dealing with. I need to be able to read them, so to speak.

On the other side of that coin, I have to be careful. In diplomatic situations, I am the face of my country, and I need to act out in my country's interest. The way I act will determine some of what they believe about my country. So I must project dignity and strength, but also friendliness and understanding. It is a balance.

One other skill that I would emphasize is the ability to interpret language. Even a language we know and understand well has to be interpreted. Getting into a play requires interpretation, and I use that skill constantly.

I appreciate your interest. You're welcome.

Monologue #44 Band Director

Hi. Welcome to the band classroom. Don't mind the warm up and practicing, I can talk over it. I believe your teacher told me that I am to tell you about the skills I learned in theatre that transfer into my career as a band director.

I must tell you that I had a lot of involvement with theatre throughout my life, but I didn't take many classes. I was almost always in the orchestra pit. In college for example, I was in demand as a musician for musicals. I enjoyed the excitement of it all. Some of my best memories involve theatre.

To me, it seems that music and theatre are so closely intertwined that it is almost impossible to separate the two.

Directing a marching band has many of the same responsibilities as directing plays. I line up the music we will be presenting in the fall by the middle of summer. That is similar to choosing a play or a season of plays. Then I choreograph the movements the band will make in time to the music. If you've ever watched a marching band, you know what I'm talking about. All the elaborate formations and marching patterns that you might see on a football field, all of that has to be planned, one step at a time.

Each musician in the band has a place, and it is all very precise. Not only do we put on stadium shows, we march in formation in parades. A parade is a visual feast, and borrowing from a theatre director's sense of vision helps make it work.

Our shows have themes. The arrangement of the songs around themes tell stories. Even in an art that seems as random as band performances, people like stories.

My theatre involvement taught me a lot about setting realistic goals and rehearsals to be sure we had reached those goals. This process, which both theatre and music use, of breaking the overall goal down into smaller incremental goals, where the progress is readily apparent and measurable, is a tool I use constantly. I believe the most important aspect of discipline is time management. Everything else seems to flow from that one skill.

Maybe the most important skill I learned was from the commitment the actors I knew had to their craft. An actor could be having a bad day, but when they were on stage, you never knew it. I realize we must be true to ourselves, but managing emotions isn't just a skill for actors. It is a hallmark of maturity. When I am teaching band and working with my band students, I owe it to them to leave my personal emotional baggage at home and invest enthusiasm and energy into the music. Not only do I practice this, I expect my students to practice it.

One other skill I would mention, and that is the art and practice of community. I have learned how to bring people together, to help them find the best parts of themselves and to see the best in others. My band students have permission to be themselves and I teach them the joy of knowing others and passing time together in a meaningful activity.

You're welcome, and I appreciate the opportunity to help. Tell your teacher I said hi.

Monologue #45 Logistician

Hi. I hope you don't mind meeting here at the docks, but this is a good place to tell you about what I do in the logistics industry and how it involves skills that I gained or honed in theatre. That's the assignment, right?

Logistics is the field of moving stuff around efficiently using different means of transportation like ships, trains, airplanes, trucks, and in some places even bicycles. It is all about managing costs and time. I am called a logistician.

I don't work for the post office, but a common example of what I do is mailing a letter to a different part of the country. You walk it out to your mailbox, that's the first step. Then a mail carrier driving a postal vehicle, picks it up and takes it to the local post office. There it is loaded with lots of other mail onto a truck. The truck takes it to a regional sorting center. The letters are sorted by zip code and loaded on trucks bound in different directions to different parts of the country. Yours is sent along with others going that direction. It arrives at another regional center, this time to be placed on a truck going to the local post office where it will then be delivered. A mail carrier similar to the one who picked it up in the first place will put it in the mailbox at the address you wrote on it.

If your letter were going to a foreign country, and if you were willing to pay a little more, then it would be flown on an airplane.

Let's say you were a busy lawyer and had some documents that needed to be signed across a busy city. Your best way to get it done might be to get someone on a bicycle who can weave through traffic and run up steps to take the documents and bring them right back.

I do logistics for a major retailer. I studied theatre in highschool, and although I did a little acting, I usually worked on the technical side of things. I cannot think of a better way to train for a logistics career. There are all these items that you have to assemble, and they can come from anywhere. That's what logistics is, getting things where they are supposed to go.

In theatre, maybe the production calls for a big bowl to place at the center of a table and you are in charge of finding one. You start asking around, and one of the actors' grandparents has just the bowl you need. Problem is, the grandparents live in a town thirty miles away, and you need the bowl for rehearsal tomorrow. So what do you do? As it so happens, your best friend's uncle works in that town thirty miles away. So you get him to bring it on his way back from work. Your best friend brings it to school and gives it to you, and you take it to the theatre.

Theatre gave me a lot of training for logistics work. One other thing I learned was from the acting side. Sometimes there are items that are in demand that have to be moved with urgency. I have to be able to communicate that to everyone in the supply line.

You're welcome. I hope you enjoy your day.

Monologue #46 Non-profit Charity Case Manager

Hi. I hope you don't mind meeting out on a public sidewalk like this, but I thought it would give you an idea of the reality that some people face. I am a case manager for a non-profit charitable organization that helps homeless families and individuals. Your teacher asked me to give you an interview about how skills I learned in theatre transfer to my work.

I took theatre courses throughout my school years and in college. I did a degree in social work in college.

Although the charity that I work for helps people who have been displaced from their homes for many reasons, we specialize in helping those whose homes have been burned.

Theatre taught me so many things about human emotions, and after a fire almost all of them will be on display. There is a profound feeling of loss and grief that family members will feel. It's not just practical items they lose. Sometimes it's family photos that go back generations. Sometimes it's gifts that remind them of people they love. And as for the practical, it's clothing and toothpaste and medications, many items that are needed immediately and sometimes it's life and death needs.

Think of the best actors you know and how they summon their most intense feelings then imagine seeing that level of feeling in real life a couple of times a month. The fire will become the event that a family will use as a point of reference forever after a home burns. The family life will be divided into "before the fire" and "since the fire." That's how dramatic it is, and I have to be able to empathise and respond to them according to what they are feeling.

It's like finding myself in the middle of a play, and I have the script which no one else has read. Suddenly I have to use some director skills. My organization owns a couple of houses where families can stay temporarily after a fire. Most families have relatives that help at that time, but some do not. That's where my organization comes in. If I do my job right, we have everything set up and waiting for them when they get there. New toothbrushes, new shoes, new clothes, a pantry full of foods, etc.

Once I am on the scene of the fire, sometimes when it is still smoldering, and when the family is still in a state of shock, I start communicating their needs to a small team. The team assembles needed items and prepares the home for the family's arrival. If the family makes arrangements to stay elsewhere, we send the items to them. Theatre is a great teacher of complex problem solving and teamwork.

One last thing I would mention. Nonprofits by their nature are in constant need of funding. The director of mine insists that we all get involved with fundraising for the organization. We have to be able to effectively communicate what we do and the need that we help fulfill. We appeal to foundations that exist to help charities. We appeal to individuals and to businesses that can help in some particular way. There is theatricality in our appeals. We try to make them feel what our victims feel. That's important.

Thank you for interviewing me.

Monologue #47 Restaurant Server

Hi, this seems like the perfect table. I wouldn't want to spoil your appetite, but we have chips and a dip we make here in the restaurant, secret recipe. I'll get some.

Here ya go. The chips are fresh baked and still hot. I understand this is an interview about how I gained some skills in theatre that I use in my job waiting tables in a restaurant.

I was in plays growing up, and I started taking theatre in middle school. It was not my choice at first. My family thought I was shy and steered me in that direction, and I'm glad they did. I gained confidence and had a good time.

And I guess that's the first skill I would mention, or at least I think of it as a skill, and that's "confidence." I think of it as a skill because it can be learned and a person can grow in confidence and then help others gain it. Like with most things, we learn by doing. Acting in plays and playing games in theatre class made me really put myself out there. I even made mistakes and failed a few times, but through those experiences I learned how to get back up and keep going.

I learned how to control my emotions and displays of emotion. No one has absolute control of their emotions, but maturity and control of emotions are about the same thing. Sooner or later, every server gets a customer who is rude. It is still a server's job to treat them with respect, to greet them pleasantly, and to thank them with a smile.

Restaurant etiquette is an unwritten script. When guests arrive, they are welcomed by a greeter who will arrange seating and lead them to a table. If guests are brought to my table, the greeter introduces me to them by name. I immediately start out by taking drink orders. Once I bring the drinks I give time for guests to decide what they like on the menu. I take the orders. I bring them what they need until they are ready to go. Hopefully the entire experience goes smoothly, and everyone is happy, and we say "thank you" and "please come back" and other such pleasantries.

In theatre I learned to memorize scripts and to act out my part with intensity. That's what etiquette is all about.

Being able to work with a "cast and crew" is another important skill in the restaurant industry. Our managers are the directors. Cooks are the crew. Greeters and servers are the actors. What I'm saying is that a restaurant functions a lot like a theatre. The similarities are obvious. Not only do I have to relate to customers, I have to communicate well with the people who work in the kitchen. The relationships are all interconnected.

The last area that I will mention is that theatre helped me gain some physical coordination, flexibility, and stamina. There are aspects of acting that are very physical, and we did training exercises to address them. We did warm up exercises and stretching exercises. I performed in a couple of musicals that gave me some extremely challenging workouts.

Well, it looks like we have customers arriving. I enjoyed meeting with you. Let me get you a bag for the rest of those chips.

Monologue #48 Documentary Maker

Hello. I hope you don't mind meeting here at a football stadium, but it's nice weather today, and you can get an idea of what I do better at a place like this, where I will be working tonight.

Your teacher told me that I am to give you an interview about the skills I learned in theatre that transfer into my work. I was told that people from many types of work would be doing these interviews. I guess mine will be one of the easiest since there is so much overlap, but stage and movie production is in some ways quite different from producing documentaries. So let me jump right into it.

I started taking theatre classes in middle school. I immediately found my place in the technical, especially operating sound and video equipment. I know that some purists in theatre don't even like the idea of making video recordings of plays, but I believe it can be helpful for an actor to watch themself practice and to critique themself. I mean, if you've got a card, play it, right? But to each their own.

I learned a lot about how to use a camera in my theatre work. I got good with focusing and knowing where the action was heading so that the camera would be there waiting a split second before the action happened. I learned a lot about editing as part of the recording and dissemination process. My school had access to computers and programs that I otherwise would not have had opportunities to use at that age. All these things quite naturally flow into what I do making documentaries.

I learned a lot about the story telling techniques of the great playwrights, but here is where things are different. A playwright uses their creativity to make up stories based on their observations. I share my literal observations in story form. A playwright starts with themes and meaning. If I do my work well, themes and meaning emerge in the process.

Let's take for example the football game I will be recording tonight. I am working on a documentary following a youth league team from an economically disadvantaged country. They will be playing for the world championship. Each team member has an individual story, and they have a story as a team. Already I am seeing themes like perseverance, innocence, joy, and how playing on the team has helped each player grow. It is really inspiring.

I will take several hundred hours of video, then I will cut and edit it into one story that will last about an hour. It will include everything from the forming of the team to each player's return to their home. I will spend about eight months in the entire process. The company that I work for will then sell it to a cable sports channel.

I have also done nature videos. Even animals participate in stories. One of my favorite things to document is music festivals. From setting up stages to taking them down, most music festivals are a story of joy.

You're welcome, and I appreciate the opportunity to speak with you.

Monologue #49 Dairy Farmer

Hi. Welcome to the farm. Here are some rubber boots that the summer camp kids wear when they visit in the summers. I'm sure there are some that will fit your feet.

Your teacher asked me to give you an interview about the skills I learned in theatre that apply to my working life as a dairy farmer. I had to give it some thought, but I believe I can help you out.

Dairy farmers take care of the cows that supply the milk that you drink with your breakfast. It also becomes things like yogurt, sour cream, whipped cream, buttermilk, condensed milk, powdered milk, ice cream, and hundreds of kinds of cheeses to name a few.

If you ask a scientist that specializes in dairy cows how to get them to give more milk, one of the first things you'll learn is that the more comfortable the cow, the more milk she gives. Stressed cows don't give much milk. So I practice comforting body language around the cows at all times and train farmworkers to do the same.

Before I go to milk the cows, I do some exercises to get myself mentally and physically relaxed. I talk to the cows as I milk them. I give them names. I sing relaxing songs to them. I pat them and anything else I can think of to make them feel loved, safe, and secure.

To help myself get relaxed I use some of the same warm up exercises I learned in theatre. The way I get in touch with real emotions and communicate those emotions to the cows, I learned that in theatre. As for the singing, well, I certainly got a lot of practice in theatre.

Dairy farming is about more than cows. There is a business side to it, and that involves relating to humans. My dairy is subject to inspection at any time by health agents. I have to keep all my milking machines and storage tanks shiny and free of any contamination. If the farm looks run down in general that will prejudice the inspectors so it is important that the entire farm look clean and healthy. In a sense it is like maintaining a theater. I have to present this farm to the eyes of the world in a way that is appealing.

Even the cows need to look healthy and energetic. Appearances matter, and I guess I'm their director.

I hire workers to help around the farm. They do things like put hay bales in storage and remove weeds from the pastures. I have found that I have to be a leader and set the pace for the work. There is an element of theatricality in that.

Finally I would mention that when I have free time, which isn't often, I like to take a walk around the farm and enjoy the show. I like to see it all running smoothly like a play where everyone knows their lines and everyone in the orchestra pit is playing in tune.

You're welcome. It's been a pleasure having you here today. Stay on this side of the fence, but go say bye to the cows before you go.

Monologue #50 Barista

Hi, and welcome to the coffee shop. Your teacher asked me to give you an interview about theatre skills that transfer into my work as a barista.

I took theatre classes in high school. I am currently a college student, majoring in business, but I am taking theatre classes when I can.

A barista is someone who makes coffee and other drinks in places like this one. Although, to be clear, I should tell you that this coffee shop is different from most. It's one of a growing number of non-profit coffee shops. We call it a "Restaria," which sounds a little bit like "rest area." We ask for donations for time spent, for beverages, and for the general upkeep of the facility. Our main purpose is to create a healthy community that helps eliminate loneliness.

I will start by telling you about some skills that help baristas in general and then tell you about some that help in this special type environment.

Coffee shop customers are drawn to the environment. It is typically a quiet and thoughtful environment. Some people go to a coffee shop to study. Some go to engage in conversation. Some go just to get out of their house or apartment. Coffee shops have a unique atmosphere, and as a barista, maintaining that atmosphere is the most important thing. Making drinks is second.

Creating and maintaining an atmosphere is a theatre skill. Every play has an ambience of its own. The ambience is the feel that usually begins to manifest near the beginning of the play. The tone of voice a barista uses, the politeness that a barista extends, even the way a barista moves helps create the atmosphere of a coffee shop.

There are other theatre skills that come into play like getting the lighting right, getting the music right. You really want the place to have a charming, friendly feel to it.

As for the coffee, there is a little bit of a show going on with making it. You really want to emphasize the sound of the steaming as you make espresso drinks. If you make a latte, which is a coffee and milk drink, there is an art to making the foam. The short, fun ritual of making a drink is a great way to break the ice with the customer. It helps put a smile on their face and relaxes them.

This particular shop requires some other skills. It is non-profit and has a mission. The mission is to build community, and what that means is I introduce people to each other based on my read of who connects best with whom. I mostly go by profession. People tend to have the most in common with others in their profession. I search for what is best in people and try to help everyone see it. My purpose is to make this a place where people really are welcomed, and even if they can't afford an expensive coffee drink, they can feel comfortable in the community that hangs out here.

Thank you for interviewing me, and you're welcome. Tell your teacher I said hi. Have a nice day.

Each Sentence/Paragraph of The Transferable Skills of Theatre is compatible with DRAMAGLOM the Acting Game!

The most basic form of DRAMAGLOM involves drawing a Cue Card, an Expression Card, and an Intensity card and acting them out simultaneously. For example, you might draw the Cue card that reads "I love you," the Expression card "Happy" and the Intensity card "Level 5 Extreme." You would read "I love you" acting out extreme happiness. Your teammate would then guess what expression and intensity you were going for to win those cards. Advanced forms of DRAMAGLOM involve transitioning between Expressions and Intensities or manifesting multiple Expressions and Intensities simultaneously.

DRAMAGLOM contains 520 cards including 410 Cue Cards with unique dramatic readings, 60 Expression cards with 20 unique expressions, and 50 Intensity cards with 5 levels of intensity, mild through extreme.

DRAMAGLOM's initial following has been drama and theatre instructors who use the game as a teaching tool. DRAMAGLOM constructively fills class time and because it is fun can be used as a reward for good class behavior. DRAMAGLOM has a growing following with theatre and game enthusiasts. DRAMAGLOM also works as a party game, an ice breaker, and as an acting warm up exercise.